SPIRAL
IMPACT

SPIRAL IMPACT

The Power to Get it Done with Grace

Karen Valencic

Niche Pressworks

Indianapolis, IN

Spiral Impact: The Power to Get It Done with Grace
[Black Belt Edition]

ISBN-13: 978-1-946533-82-1 (eBook)
          978-1-946533-83-8 (Paperback)
          978-1-946533-84-5 (Hardback)

For permission to reprint portions of this content or bulk purchases, contact: info@karenvalencic.com.

Published by Niche Pressworks; http://NichePressworks.com

*Communication
creates movement;
Stillness fosters clarity;
To be moving and clear...
This is true power.*

—KAREN VALENCIC

*Dedicated to
all who desire to communicate and live
in a way that honors and brings
forth the best in people.*

*And to
Kylie, Taylor, and Dan*

CONTENTS

CONTENTS

FOREWORD

THE MODERN WORLD RADICALLY SHIFTED in 2007 when the iPhone, YouTube, Twitter, Kindle, Watson (Artificial Intelligence), and my own Spiral Impact were launched, along with many other social platforms and technologies. Thirteen years later, it's hard to imagine life before them. The modern world of technology continues to exponentially speed up as Moore's Law so eloquently predicted in 1965. (Moore predicted processing power would double the speed of technology every two years.)

"So, what does that matter?" you may be thinking as you read this book about human performance and communication.

It matters because humans' ability to adapt is lagging way behind the continual technological advances. While many of you don't need a graph to realize this, I was struck by this dramatic comparison of human adaptability and technology over time from Thomas Friedman's book, *Thank You for Being Late*. Friedman shares a graph by Astro Teller, CEO of Google X's "Moonshot Factory" (Friedman, 2016):

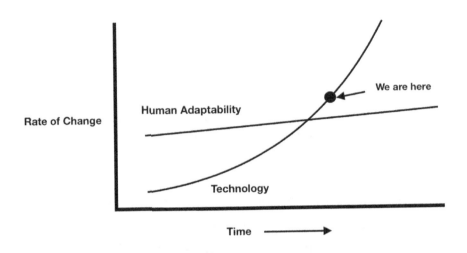

As you can see, we are beyond the crossing point, and this lag opens Pandora's Box for destructive conflict, burnout, and division. Our individual ability to bring forth our true power, master the art of conflict, and foster collaboration and civility all greatly impact our individual sense of freedom and engagement in our lives.

I've labeled this updated version of Spiral Impact, The Black Belt Edition because, contrary to most people's belief that it signifies an endpoint, a black belt signifies a new beginning, a new level of mastery after many years of practice. Preparing for a black belt test demands an accelerated and dedicated focus and practice. I believe this is true for human performance as well. The personal and professional advantages for this are where freedom and satisfaction are found.

Just like a black belt in the art I represent, *aikido*, there aren't short cuts. It's not a weekend course that you give lip service to. It requires consistent practice and a willingness to surrender old ways of doing things. The concepts in this book are simple and entirely worth the investment of your attention and time. This book is filled with nuggets to help you master conflict and feel more freedom and control in your life.

The book's subtitle *The Power to Get It Done with Grace* is standing the test of time. You may think Power and Grace in the same sentence are contradictory, partly because you may have been led to believe something different about power.

With three decades of consistent practice in *aikido*, I know that understanding the difference between power and force is a key to getting out of struggle, both on the mat and in your life.

The first time I witnessed an *aikido* demonstration, it profoundly revealed how to generate True Power, as opposed to using force, to realize one's purpose. Since that first demonstration, I have moved and fallen and spiraled my way through layers of learning.

When I began my *aikido* practice, I felt somewhat like a shrinking violet. When there were differences of perspective or intensity of emotion, I'd vacillate between withdrawing and passive-aggressively fighting. Both choices caused me to feel at the mercy of whoever or whatever held "power." Rarely did I leave the interaction feeling good and certainly not powerful.

As a young engineer I saw these dynamics play out daily in my corporate job. I wondered: What if people could come to work and honorably engage with True Power? What if we could be heard by, and value, each other? What if I, personally, could put self-doubt away and teach others to do the same? The workplace could become a positive growth environment instead of a battlefield of ego.

That is when I decided to shift careers and apply both the blending, or *ai*, and the energy, or *ki*, experienced in *aikido*, eventually creating the Spiral Impact method for generating True Power and mastering conflict, both for individuals and teams.

While learning is a never-ending spiral, I pause now to share three things I've learned about True Power and how it relates to teams and the people responsible for leading them.

1. POWER AND FORCE ARE OFTEN CONFUSED

Power is rotational; force is a straight line. Force only works when you are in a dominant position whether physically, emotionally, or positionally. Using force usually produces a short-term gain with a long-term loss.

Unfortunately, sometimes people in "positions of power" will use force to maintain or fulfill their purpose. Force divides and diminishes people. Anyone who has felt marginalized by a government, a boss, a co-worker, or a spouse knows this full well. Examples of force are: "telling" instead of "asking," deciding without consulting, and withholding key information. Force results in a push-pull interaction and may either be externally expressed or internally felt.

By contrast, True Power engages by creating positive connection through clear intent, inquiry, and acknowledgment. Power moves *with* rather than *against.*

2. POWER IS NOT ABOUT SIZE OR POSITION

As a woman I can't usually use force in *aikido* because I don't have the muscle strength to compel my stronger male partners to move. But this is an advantage, as it requires me to find leverage through my center and connection. If I were stronger, I might be tempted to use force and ultimately do harm to myself or my opponent.

The same is true in everyday life—with centering, inquiry, and clear honorable intent you create leverage. This generates True Power which can dissipate destructive force.

When rotational movement happens around a calm center, that is power. Think of a hurricane: The more defined and calm the eye, the more power it wields. It is this spiraling power of a hurricane — the same spiraling power I experience in *aikido* — that informs and extends my Spiral Impact Method.

Today, there is a trend toward teaching mindfulness and emotional intelligence in business. This is exciting to see because both require a strong *center.* These practices complement each other. Centering aligns the mind, the emotions, and the gut (instinct) for clarity.

3. TRUE POWER TAKES LESS EFFORT

As the world rapidly changes, agility and resilience are essential survival skills, and they are integral to *aikido* (on the mat) and the gift of applying the Spiral Impact method (in life). True Power minimizes resistance for increased momentum. When you 'move with' and spiral there is no resistance and momentum is released! Accomplish more, effortlessly—it is magical.

As I tie my black belt, I feel honored that it was passed on to me from two of my teachers. Without their dedication to practice and sharing what they've learned about the true nature of power, I would not be where I am today. Much appreciation to Tom Crum, who introduced me to *aikido* in that first demonstration. And to my home dojo teachers George Bevins, Joe Lavelle, and David Johnson and all the others with whom I've trained over the years.

In practical terms, I'd like you to think about what "black belt" you are working toward. It's that thing you want to master. And recognize there is no end to your practice. Receiving a black belt is actually a beginning to the next level. As you'll see soon the spiral goes on indefinitely. At the point of this writing I approach my third *aikido* black belt test. Each one, from my experience, becomes more relaxed and fun, even as it becomes more challenging.

Let's roll!
Karen

SECTION 1

INTRODUCTION

MOMENTUM INTERRUPTED

"KEEP MOVING AND BEND YOUR KNEES." These words echo in my head whenever I begin to struggle. Moving naturally reduces resistance and bending knees lowers your center of gravity for stability and flexibility.

In the early days of my martial arts practice, I would frequently feel overwhelmed by my big, sweaty opponents. If I suddenly appeared immobilized by my opponent's greater strength, my teacher's voice in the background would ring out, "Keep moving and bend your knees."

The martial art *aikido* mimics life. Movement gives us energy and creativity; struggle and fear make us feel stuck. The choices you make either create or stop momentum, both on the *aikido* practice mat and in life and work. "Keep moving and bend your knees" in everyday life means be flexible and ask questions for continuous learning.

I was initially drawn to study *aikido* from a desire to be strong, clear, and balanced, particularly in challenging situations. As a project engineer, I frequently felt frustrated and disempowered when our project team disagreed on how to proceed. When I worked in manufacturing, the pressure created by balancing quality with keeping

3

the production line moving was overwhelming at times. The dollars lost for every minute the line shut down were huge. And having my office across the hall from the union office didn't create a peaceful sanctuary to recharge in! I felt anything but balanced.

Escaping these circumstances to have children didn't lighten the stress. Taking care of a colicky infant who cried endlessly for six months was probably one of the most challenging times of my life. I wanted to be in command of my life rather than allowing circumstances to control me. *Aikido* practice develops body, mind, and spirit. As one becomes proficient in *aikido*, the skills easily transfer to all aspects of life. An increased ability to deal with conflict and influence outcomes is also a wonderful benefit.

Practice on the mat typically consists of one person providing the energy, or attack, and the other person learning to respond. In life, potential attackers or opponents may be:

Differences between people, when
- "They" just won't see things your way
- You are at an impasse in a negotiation

Demands on your time, when you
- Are over-committed
- Are feeling burned out
- Can't say "no" to others' requests
- Feel a loss of motivation before a large project is finished

Disappointments, when
- Potential clients or employers keep saying "no"
- You don't have something you want
- Unwanted change happens

Each of these scenarios has the potential to interrupt your momentum to get "it," your desired outcome, done. Using the core concepts from *aikido*, you can accomplish your "it" with power and grace. Grace in this context is beauty, finesse, and style.

In *aikido* you learn that power comes from connecting with and moving in the same direction as your opponent's attack. Therefore,

Strength comes from position, not force.

The intention of *aikido* is to protect both the attacker's life as well as your own. When practiced correctly, there is no struggle or conflict; all life is nurtured and protected. I believe mastering these principles is the path not only to creating and sustaining momentum but ultimately to freedom.

...mastering these principles is the path not only to creating and sustaining momentum but ultimately to freedom.

The problem is, differences, demands, and disappointments often create conflict. People tend to have one of five desires about conflict.

1. **MANAGE OR RESOLVE CONFLICT**—Conflict management or resolution is a popular topic in the performance improvement industry. These words imply a need to get rid of conflict or control it in some way.

2. **LOVE CONFLICT**—Some people delight in creating conflict, then watching the chaos that ensues. Often, this disengages others in significant ways.

3. **HATE CONFLICT AND AVOID IT AT ALL COSTS**—Many people fall into this category and many TV sitcoms are based upon people avoiding conflict. In the real world, it's anything but funny. The cost of doing this can be astronomical emotionally, physically, and financially.

4. **BELIEVE THEY HAVE NO CONFLICT**—Frequently people in authority positions have this belief. Often, they may not recognize (or want to recognize) the conflict happening around them.

5. **MASTER CONFLICT**—A few, rare individuals have the expectation that there will be conflict and embody the principles to embrace it, explore differences, and remove resistance. Conflict mastery requires not only that you acknowledge conflict's existence but also that you allow it to act as a catalyst for making healthy change, strengthening relationships, and creating innovation.

This is living the Spiral Impact Method! When you master conflict, you are on the path to freedom.

The concepts in this book come from 29 years of *aikido* practice and 28 years of helping people work together in a variety of circumstances. A great deal of my work has focused on conflict. Because conflict often keeps our desired outcome, our "it," out of reach, I'd like to address conflict here. Mishandled conflict often slows down and even stops momentum. Conflict is inevitable, natural and necessary for innovation, so mastering it is crucial for anyone wanting to be truly free. If that sounds a little daunting, remember that *mastery* doesn't equate to *perfection*. In his book, *Mastery: The Keys to Success and Long-Term Fulfillment*, George Leonard[1] gives us this encouragement:

> *"Mastery is not perfection, but rather*
> *a journey and the true master must be*
> *willing to try and fail and try again."*

Let's begin with an exploration of what conflict really is.

---

1   Leonard, 1991

CONFLICT DEFINED

WHEN I ASK PEOPLE WHAT CONFLICT IS, most of the time they respond with, "A difference in opinion." Conflict is not a difference in opinion; it is how we respond to a difference in opinion.

Differences are a good thing. In organizations if everyone agreed on everything, progress would stagnate. If we agreed on everything in relationships, they would be boring. We need differences to innovate and grow. For example, the difference between the tech-obsessed person and the tech-resistant person is a healthy difference. As the two share their different comfort levels and needs about technology, they both grow. The tech-obsessed person may learn he needs to adjust his ideas to fit the softer relationship needs of the company, and the tech-resistant person may learn he needs to grow in his comfort level with technology.

A difference becomes a conflict when you choose to push against the difference. The word *conflict* is derived from the Latin root words *com*, meaning *together*, and *fligere*, meaning *to strike*. So conflict means *to strike together*. Conflict can be experienced as creative tension or destructive tension. In the above example, destructive conflict could happen if the tech-obsessed person forces a point of view that technology is the answer to everything, and the tech-resistant person dismisses technology as a waste of time. When either person takes the position that he is right and the other is wrong, and then pushes his point of view beyond the comfort level of the other person, conflict becomes destructive.

Let's explore another example: Two people may have different opinions about how to grill chicken. One person may see this as merely interesting—a difference. Another person may choose to make the difference a big issue arguing that his way is right. A third observer may say nothing but feel internal conflict over his friends' arguing. A discussion, even an intense one, over how to grill chicken may or may not become destructive conflict for the two friends. Likewise, the third friend observing may or may not be bothered by the exchange.

The chicken example illustrates beautifully how conflict is an art. People experience a common event or circumstance and perceive it very differently based on their background, knowledge, and personality type.

People choose to turn differences into conflict for many reasons: past unresolved issues between those involved, learned behavior patterns, insecurity, or fear. Regardless of the reason, recognizing the behavior is the first step to changing it.

People experience a common event or circumstance and perceive it very differently based on their background, knowledge, and personality type.

Take a moment and try this: Make a fist with each of your hands. Now push them together.

Imagine this same tension pushing against another person, an event, a thing, or yourself.

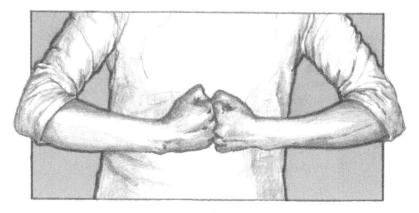

FIGURE 1: *Pushing Tension*

A certain amount of tension is creative, causing you to "move off being stuck" and find solutions. This is good. However, each person has a limit to the amount of tension he can handle before the tension becomes destructive conflict, felt internally and/or expressed externally.

When people feel pushed in any way, they almost always push back. This is Newton's Third Law: For every action there is an equal and opposite reaction. Identifying whether you are productively pushing or destructively *forcing* is crucial to mastering conflict and maintaining momentum. When you increase the push or force beyond a person's tolerance you may:

- Cause the other person to resist more, resulting in destructive conflict

11

- Shut the other person down mentally, emotionally, or physically
- Cause yourself to burn out or collapse

The secret to truly mastering conflict is to understand and honor the different people involved in the process. Recognizing how much tension or pushing is productive, given the people involved, is key to mastering conflict.

DESTRUCTIVE CONFLICT
Pushes too hard, too fast, or too long
The intention is to control, make wrong, or destroy

CONFLICT MASTERY
Pushes just right for the people involved
The intention to is engage for positive outcome and innovation

---

In *aikido* practice, conflict is required. Sensitivity to how much physical power your practice partner can take is crucial to helping her learn. As she develops her skills, the more physical intensity she can handle.

Only one of the people involved in the conflict must make a different choice to create movement rather than an impasse. This is also true for many of my clients, as illustrated by the following story.

At wit's end, Hank called me for advice. He felt defeated and bewildered. Hank's agency provides educational materials for health clinics. Providing the information contained in the materials is a standard state requirement. Hank's service saves the clinic's resources they would otherwise need to purchase to create their own materials. Yet, the first two meetings with clinic staff were like a battle. Why were these people so resistant?

After asking Hank a series of questions, I had a sense the people may have felt Hank was "pushing" his agenda. Even though they needed and wanted the materials, they felt pushed and were subtly pushing back.

I suggested he go back in with the intention of learning all he could about them, asking questions rather than giving them solutions. Before he met with them, he was also to do some deep breathing and relax a little.

Hank reported back that his next meeting felt almost too easy. He had asked questions and listened. His customers were then very open to what he had to offer. Hank's changed approach changed their response. He got his desired outcome.

When change or disappointment happens, you can struggle internally or "keep moving and bend your knees," as in the next example:

It was a very long night flying back from South America. Sleeping in a foreign airport made us all a little on edge by the time we landed in Dallas at 5:30 AM.

Two women from NYC were anxious about returning on time for appointments scheduled that day. As we deplaned, we all scrambled toward the flight schedule to learn the status of our connections. The two NYC travelers learned their flight was canceled. One woman sat down full of despair, totally debilitated by the news. The other woman immediately began to scan the other airlines' flights. She saw another flight to New York, which was scheduled to arrive earlier than their original flight. She moved quickly to secure a seat on the flight, and away she went. She kept moving and bent her knees. She got "it" done with grace—and even included the other woman in her solution.

The way you choose to interact with people can create a lot of conflict and unnecessary work for yourself. "Keep moving and bend your knees" applies here as well.

Ingrid felt invincible; she was a smart, capable person. She knew how to "get it done." The trouble for her employer was that she had no grace in her style. Her way was the right way; she shut down and disempowered others in the organization. She was in command and control, giving little respect to most of the people she worked with. She did, however, get small project results, which made her valuable to the organization.

Mid-career she was awarded responsibility for a multi-million-dollar global project. This was the opportunity of a lifetime. Her superiors knew she had the knowledge needed for the project. They also knew and were concerned about her ability to lead effectively; they knew Ingrid's command and control style could potentially alienate the project team.

Ingrid and I spent quite a bit of time building communication skills at the onset of the project. She began to see the importance of everyone's working together. When I demonstrated the concept of "keep moving and bend your knees," she literally experienced, through the aikido movement, how much easier it was to work with people rather than constantly direct and control them. She ultimately saw the value of leading by bringing out the best in people rather than shutting them down. As I facilitated several team development sessions, Ingrid enjoyed the team interaction and reaped the benefits of a group working together. She verbalized she was relieved to have the cooperative support of the team, rather than having to follow every detail herself.

A few months passed, and I met again with Ingrid. She told me everything was going well if she kept a constant watch over everyone. Seeing my face drop, with wide eyes she sighed, "I'm still trying to command and control, aren't I?" The pressure to succeed had caused her to resort to old behavior, which was paralyzing and, again, alienating the team. Her behavior was also draining her energy and time. She needed to shift back to "keep moving and bend her knees" to keep the team engaged. We created a strategy that included ongoing coaching and daily reminders, both visual and auditory, to keep her on track.

Ingrid's project was ultimately successful. When last we talked, she was taking on an even larger leadership role in the organization.

I've learned over the years that whenever I feel stuck or like I'm pushing, I "keep moving and bend my knees." This is how to create the power to get it done with grace.

A BRIEF HISTORY OF AIKIDO

Aikido is a fairly new martial art. It was created in the mid-twentieth century by a Japanese man named Morihei Ueshiba. Mr. Ueshiba, also referred to as O Sensei or "Great Teacher," is considered by many people to be one of the finest martial artists of all time. He studied and mastered many different martial arts. O Sensei created a new and somewhat radical martial arts philosophy that became aikido. Unlike most other martial arts, aikido reflects O Sensei's desire to experience conflict in a way that honors, rather than destroys, life.

Aikido is not a defensive martial art. It is an art of self-development. Learning to maintain your sense of self and power while simultaneously honoring the other person is a difficult task. Learning the art of aikido requires many years of practice. Occasionally, people use the term "verbal aikido." Aikido cannot be done verbally. The art requires integration of body/mind/spirit to truly be effective.

The intention of this book is to apply the concepts of aikido to everyday life.

To see a couple of great aikido videos go to:

www.karenvalencic.com/resources/

To learn more about *aikido*, specifically, I suggest the following books:

Principles of Aikido by Mitsugi Saotome

Aikido and the Harmony of Nature by Mitsugi Saotome

THE
SPIRAL IMPACT® METHOD

THE SPIRAL IMPACT PROCESS

THE GOOD NEWS IS you don't have to become an *aikido* master or even take the first step into a martial arts *dojo*, or place of practice, to learn the concepts required to generate the power to get your "it" done with grace. The Spiral Impact methodology provides you with the process to use the principles in your everyday life.

In this section you'll learn about the process of generating power with grace, using The Spiral Impact Model's four Quadrants:

- **THE KNOWLEDGE QUADRANT**—Knowing Yourself, Understanding Others (It), and Us
- **THE FOCUSED ENERGY QUADRANT**—Being the Calm Eye of the Storm
- **THE INTENTION QUADRANT**—Defining Your Desired Outcome
- **THE SUPPORT QUADRANT**—Securing Help

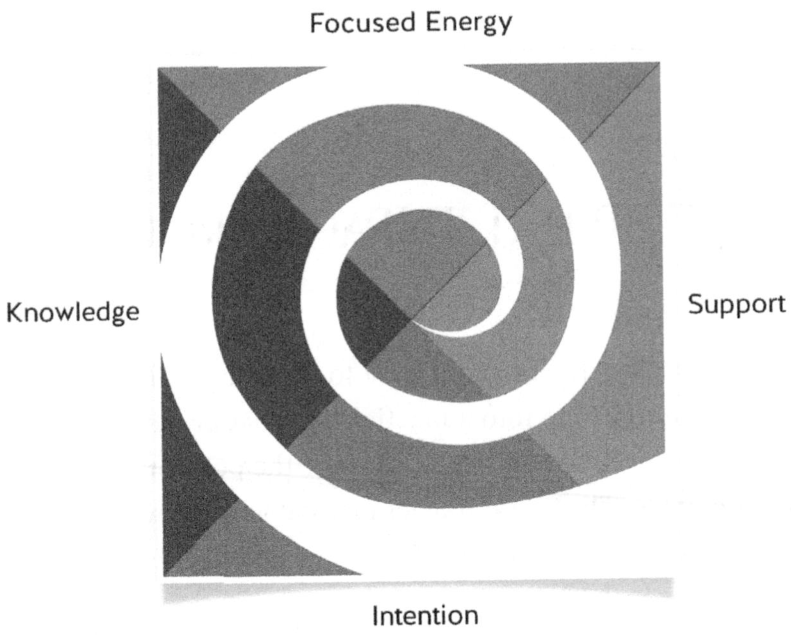

Focused Energy

Knowledge

Support

Intention

FIGURE 2: *Spiral Impact Quadrants*

THE SPIRAL IMPACT MODEL

GENERATING POWER WITH GRACE

"Magic" describes my first impression of a master *aikido* teacher in action. Several attackers rushed him and were propelled away by what seemed a very slight movement in his hips and wrists, unleashing a powerful invisible force field. Initially, I thought it must be an act. The attackers were not really trying. Over time I've come to know it was no act.

As you become proficient in *aikido*, when you feel attacked, you simply move into and with the force in a spiral, eliminating the struggle. Your movement causes the attacker to lose balance and shift position as well. Your intention is not to avoid or leave an attack situation; it is to shift your body and move in the same direction as the attacker's force. The more advanced the practitioner, the more internal and subtle the movement.

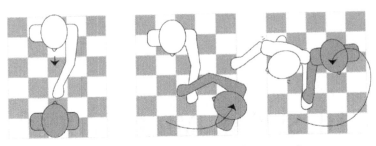

FIGURE 3: *Spiraling in toward an attack*

This concept is simple and effective, if counter-intuitive, to Western culture's tendency to dominate, destroy, or avoid in conflict situations.

Somehow in our busy and stressed-out Western world, we have acquired the notion that high performance results from the philosophy of, as the familiar Nike brand says, "Just Do It." Jumping in with a direct attack in "just do it" fashion is exciting! Health club attendance in January, due to New Year's resolutions, is a great example of "just do it." Falling attendance in March is an example of how a long-term result requires something more.

"Just do it" applied to a difference or conflict might mean just telling it like it is, without regard to the other person's feelings or perspectives ("brutal" honesty). But the long-term fallout of this approach may be a loss of trust or of the relationship itself. "Just do it" might also suggest leaving a situation suddenly, missing the lessons available there or the opportunity to make the situation better.

If you look to nature, power—the capacity to get work done—is greatest when it moves in a spiral motion.

While just doing it may work in the short term to get us excited, in the long run, it may fall short. If you look to nature, power—the capacity to get work done—is greatest when it moves in a spiral motion. If you've ever seen a hurricane or tornado, you've seen that spiral motion. There is much more power generated by a tornado than by a strong, linear wind gale.

The strength of spiral motion is also demonstrated by the difference between driving a nail versus a screw. Joining two medium-density boards with a nail requires focused, intense force; this "just do it" approach works well in simple situations. But if you're working with less stable material (plaster, brick, etc.) or very hard wood, or if the nail and boards are not perfectly lined up, you end up with a bent nail, bruised fingers, and an unsatisfactory result. On the other hand, driving a screw requires less brute force and provides better stability. More importantly, over time, when subjected to vibration, moisture, and temperature changes, the screw will maintain the connection better with the increased holding power resulting from the greater surface area contact and angles provided by its threads.

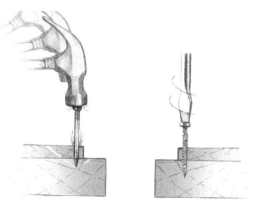

FIGURE 4: *Force vs. Spiral Power*

We can learn from the nail and screw as they apply to dealing with differences, demands, and disappointments. Spiral Impact harnesses the power of the spiral to maintain momentum, minimize burnout by requiring less force, and generate strength and stability for the long haul.

Throwing someone twice your size across the room is surprisingly easy when a spiral is applied. Almost all *aikido* technique is based on spiral movement. Even when taking a fall, the spiral is employed to soften the impact and propel you back to your feet quickly.

The Spiral Impact Method was born during my fifteenth year of *aikido* practice. I've gradually come to realize that all human performance is about process and cycles, not one-time forced events. Even though *aikido* might look graceful and fluid like a dance, great power is clearly generated through the spiral movement.

Hence, Spiral Impact is a methodology that honors the natural power cycle of nature: the spiral. The ability to maintain momentum with power and grace is realized with these concepts.

When Spiral Impact becomes second nature, it may look to others like we are "just doing it" because the results appear instantaneous and easy. In fact, it's sometimes easy, even for me, to lose sight of the power of my process.

"How did you make this radical change in careers, from employment as an engineer in a huge corporation to small business

owner teaching conflict resolution? How did you do it? Did you 'just do it?'"

I was a little taken aback by his question. On one hand it felt like I, in fact, "just did it." On the other hand, "just do it" seemed to negate the process I went through. What I did "just do" was make a decision to create a viable business helping people work together; the process of actually doing it was the Spiral Impact process. Spiral Impact provided the momentum through the tough times for me to reach my goal.

For example, each time I became discouraged, I'd either revisit my intention, find a supportive person to talk with, seek resources to increase my business acumen and subject-matter knowledge, or take time out and re-focus my energy through breathing, exercising, or just taking a break.

Recognizing that achieving big business growth every day is an unrealistic expectation and having strategies to continue to nurture the business internally when external growth wasn't apparent, were the keys to my success.

> **When you apply Spiral Impact, it feels like you "just did it" because the results are easy and long-lasting.**

People frequently give up on an idea or a relationship when it gets too hard or they feel stuck. They start struggling. At that point the key to continued momentum toward the goal is to do something different. This is accomplished by Quadrant Shifting on the Spiral Impact Model.

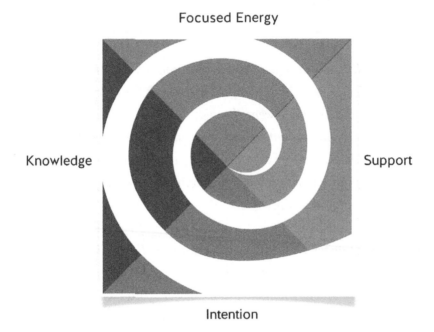

FIGURE 5: *Spiral Impact Quadrants*

The Spiral Impact Model is composed of quadrants shown in Figure 4. Quadrant Shifting around the spiral generates momentum. One quadrant has no advantage over the others, and one by itself has little power to create your desired outcome, whether it be building a business, a house, a team, or a great relationship.

WHAT IS POWER?

The phrase "knowledge is power" is frequently used by newspapers, libraries, and educational institutions. I challenge this statement. I believe knowledge by itself has no power. *Applied* knowledge, however, has great power.

How many things do you *know* are important to do, yet you do not *do* them? Consider the following:

- We have vast amounts of knowledge about the effect of diet and exercise on wellness—yet look at the declining health of so many of us.
- We've all heard how important follow-up is in business—but how many excuses do we make for not picking up the phone?
- We know we should back up the data on our computers—yet do we?
- We know how important writing a will is—yet many of us pass on, leaving families without the protection of one.

Power is the rate at which work is done. Spiral Impact transforms knowledge into power by adding intention, focused energy, and support, which gives our knowledge momentum and, therefore, life.

As shown in Figure 4, above, we generate momentum by moving around the spiral. For example, if you want to lose weight, having the knowledge is just one part of the process. Having a clear picture or intention of your desired outcome is also of extreme importance. Enlisting support, such as a coach, is another part that adds power to create the desired outcome. And focusing your energy through meditation or breathing adds still more power. It's a continual process. You have to gather knowledge about different strategies for losing weight, revisit your intention daily, find ways to support your intentions, and practice focusing your energy daily.

Making a decision? Quadrant Shift around the entire spiral to ensure you are making a solid decision. Mastering a conflict? Quadrant Shift around the entire spiral to make sure you have clarity for a great resolution. Involved in a long-term project? Quadrant Shift to each element to gain clarity and minimize burnout along the way. In short: When you feel stuck, Quadrant Shift.

There is no right beginning place or necessarily any particular order to these quadrants. However, it is important to visit all of them.

The following four segments explore the elements of each quadrant and share tips for activating each quadrant. Section 3: "Spiral Impact in Action," offers examples for applying the model to a variety of general life circumstances. Section 4: "Take Spiral Impact to the Mat for Business" explores application to business issues.

> **"Life is like riding a bicycle. To keep your balance you must keep moving."** –EINSTEIN

Power comes with responsibility. The Spiral Impact concept generates personal power. The intention behind the power you generate is crucial to your long-term success. If you use it to manipulate, or use others to your advantage, it will backfire—guaranteed.

> *"I bet you could beat up anyone in this room."* I hear this frequently when people learn of my martial arts practice... it always surprises me.
>
> *(Maybe I could, but I won't.)*

As my skills in aikido are developed, so is my capacity to do harm. However, developing confidence, awareness, intuition, and personal responsibility are the intentions of my practice. The discipline is to know you could, but you don't.

All of us find ourselves in positions of power over someone else. We could exert that power and do harm, but we don't. For example:

- In traffic, you could become aggressive, but you don't.
- As a co-worker, you could participate in gossip, but you don't.
- As a boss, you could take advantage of an employee's time, but you don't.
- As a parent, you could yell at a child, but you don't.

The longer I practice, the more I find that not only won't I harm others, but I also cannot because doing so goes against my very nature.

> *"Nearly all men can stand adversity, but if you want to test a man's character, give him power."* –ABRAHAM LINCOLN

Next, we'll take a closer look at each Quadrant in the Spiral Impact Model.

ACTIVATING SPIRAL IMPACT

1. **READ THIS BOOK** through to the end.

2. **AT THE END OF EACH OF THE FOUR QUADRANT SEGMENTS,** there is an "activation" page. This page contains suggestions to activate that particular Quadrant.

3. **WHEN YOU FEEL STUCK** or in a struggle Quadrant Shift to create momentum.

4. **REFER TO SECTION 3,** Spiral Impact in Action for specific application maps and examples.

5. **REMEMBER** to "keep moving and bend your knees!"

THE KNOWLEDGE QUADRANT

GETTING TO KNOW YOURSELF, OTHERS (OR IT), AND US

Hindsight is always 20/20. Making a deliberate effort to understand others and gain knowledge *before* you take action will greatly sharpen your foresight. In the effort to create quick results, jumping too fast into action can be a big mistake costing time, money, and relationships. Knowledge is essential to getting "it" done with power and grace.

In this Quadrant, you'll learn about:

- KNOWING YOURSELF—Identify your typical response to obstacles
- UNDERSTANDING OTHERS OR IT—Inquire to learn about the other person, group or thing
- UNDERSTANDING US—Notice the change of behavior when a group forms
- ACTIVATING THE KNOWLEDGE QUADRANT—Tips for increasing knowledge and understanding

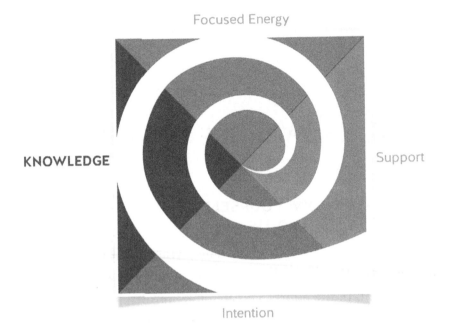

Focused Energy

KNOWLEDGE

Support

Intention

FIGURE 6: *Spiral Impact Quadrants Emphasis on Knowledge*

KNOWING YOURSELF

Aikido practitioners, especially beginners, quickly discover that their instinctive reaction to a threat comes out on the training mat. Typically, they either give up too easily or fight too hard, lacking power *and* grace. Over years of observation, I have noticed that the way someone interacts on the mat mirrors how they respond in everyday life under pressure.

TAKE THE VISION PATH

Every significant interaction you have in life either increases or diminishes your energy, influence, and balance. This is true whether the interaction is with a person, an event, or a thing—for example, the team member who doesn't follow through on commitments, a significant unexpected rise in taxes, or a frozen computer. How you interact is always your choice, and this choice directly affects your ability to get your life's activities done with grace.

When you are not getting what you want, knowing yourself is the beginning of making different choices. Then combining your self-knowledge with actions suggested by the Spiral Impact Model's other Quadrants—declaring your intention, engaging support, and focusing your energy—helps you make conscious decisions to handle most challenging situations.

We all have patterns of interaction we continually repeat. Einstein's definition of insanity is doing the same thing over and over and expecting a different result.

To illustrate this, bring to mind a particular situation that you'd like to be different from what it is currently. This could be a conflict with someone, an undesired life circumstance, or an unattained goal.

Now consider: What is this situation preventing you from having? What is your desired outcome? This is your "it."

YOU  **YOUR "IT"**

Your "it" can be something as simple as having a nice day or getting to work on time, or as complex as building a multi-million-dollar company, reorganizing a department, or having a fabulous relationship. Just be sure your "it" is not about a specific person doing something. Consider the result you want.

Now write down your "it," the desired outcome that seems out of reach because of the situation you identified above. You will refer to this later.

Now, imagine you are standing, ready to walk to your "it," a mere 20 feet in front of you. Isn't it great when you can just walk to "it" and get there without a hitch?

In life, obstacles often come up, blocking easy passage to your "it." Your idea to improve a product design is rebuffed by the financial department because of cost; your easy trip to the office gets delayed by an unexpected accident in traffic; your child gets sick the day of your big presentation and can't go to daycare. The list is endless.

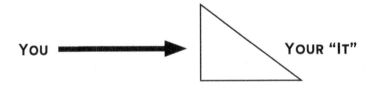

How you choose to interact with an obstacle increases or diminishes your energy, influence, and balance.

In my seminars, I ask people what obstacles specifically get in the way of having what they want right now. Some typical responses are:

- Other people's agendas
- Other people's attitudes
- Fear
- Too much to do
- Not enough money

- Lack of health
- System or process issues
- Lack of knowledge

Now I'll ask you: What gets in *your* way?

And, more importantly, what do you do to deal with this obstacle? Think about this from a physical standpoint. If your obstacle were an actual object in front of you, what options would you have to physically get past the obstacle?

Figure 7, a flowchart of The Vision Path, illustrates your interaction choices. What choice do you typically make? What choice are you currently making in the situation you identified above?

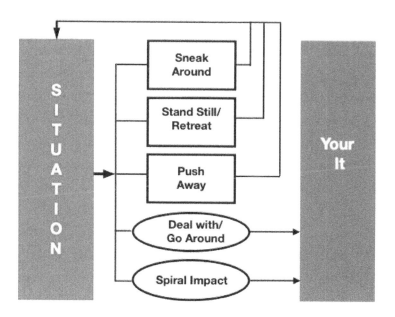

FIGURE 7: *The Vision Path*

Here are the five most common options people choose:
SNEAKING AROUND. Or avoiding dealing with the situation, perhaps adopting passive-aggressive behavior. This happens often in large organizations when people don't know how to communicate. Triangulation is also a form of sneaking around, which is involving a third party rather than directly with the person. Credit cards are a great example of "sneaking around" money issues. Excessive drinking and eating are ways we sneak around emotional issues.

STANDING STILL OR RETREATING. This choice obviously does not move us toward our desired outcome, our "it." Sometimes standing still is wise, say, if you are waiting for more information or the correct time.

You must distinguish whether you are standing still as avoidance or for correct timing.

PUSHING AWAY. Or forcing an outcome. This choice often takes the form of yelling or dominating others. Typically, these behaviors are self-defeating; they may give us a short-term victory but a long-term loss: We may get our way but alienate the other person. We don't really resolve issues when we force an outcome, and often it makes things worse. This is true when we interact with physical objects, too. Ever try to fix a computer by pushing buttons out of frustration? Did you end up with a bigger mess than you had in the beginning?

DEALING WITH OR GOING AROUND. Or addressing the issue in a constructive way, and then moving around it. Examples, especially when an obstacle involves another person, include:

- **COMPROMISE.** This is frequently the first suggestion when the obstacle is a conflict between people. Remember, when you compromise, both parties give up something. Compromise works best with issues that are not that important to you or for a short-term solution. Compromising for a long-term, significant solution usually does not work.
- **AGREE TO DISAGREE.** This requires two emotionally mature people; otherwise, it ends poorly.
- **MEDIATE.** A third party can often help to facilitate discussion.
- **TELL YOUR TRUTH** about the situation in an honorable way.
- **FIND PEACE WITHIN.** Some situations have no resolution other than internal acceptance. Often people work to try to change an impossible situation or another person. Typically, you can't change other people. However, changing your own behavior changes how they behave toward you. While what we resist persists, often when we truly "let it go," the obstacle goes away.

USING SPIRAL IMPACT. Take the obstacle along with you, in a sense, by embracing the situation for what you can learn from it and discover alternative creative solutions for creating momentum. Examples include having an honest conversation with a perceived adversary, which can take your relationship to another, better level; or seeing your competition as an ally for mutual benefit. Each Quadrant in the Model offers an opportunity to "Spiral Impact" the situation. This concept is covered in detail in the final section of this book.

. . . .

Sometimes people will comment in my seminars, "Just change your 'it!'" If the obstacles are insurmountable, you may, in fact, decide to change your desired outcome—though I encourage you not to give up too easily!

Changing the desired outcome merely puts you in another situation where different obstacles exist. You could change your "it" and find yourself facing the same challenges. You'll always need to look at your interactive behavior and determine if you need to change your approach.

Everywhere you go, there you are.
Changing your "it" may not be necessary
if you hone your interaction skills.

"He is such a jerk," lamented Aaron, one of my students, about his boss. "He is constantly changing his mind after I've completed a project. Then I have to start all over. I love this company; I hate this situation. Why do they promote such incompetent, flaky people?"

Knowing that standing still, pushing, or sneaking around the situation would not work, Aaron tried all kinds of communication techniques with his boss to make his situation better. Things didn't change. Eventually Aaron came to terms with the fact that if he wanted to stay with this company, his boss's behavior was part of the picture. While he continued to explore opportunities in other departments and improve his job-specific skills, he truly "let go" of trying to change his boss. I remember distinctly when he shared this with me. He had really turned a corner.

Guess what happened then? His boss left the company rather suddenly. I've seen these types of situations happen over and over again. What we resist persists. Often when we let it go— it goes away!

You can't change other people. You can only change yourself. That is good news because the only person you can control is you.

I arrived an hour early, stunned to see that the room was set for two hundred. Initially, I felt overwhelmed. How was I going to transform this room into an intimate seminar with 20 people? Showtime was in 50 minutes.

I went through my list of options, referring to The Vision Path. **Standing still** *was not an option.* **Pushing it away,** *which looked like rushing to move all the tables and chairs, was not a viable option either; I had a knee injury and could not.* **Sneaking around** *didn't apply.* **Dealing with then going around it** *wasn't possible either since there was no one around to deal with.*

Using Spiral Impact, or Spiral Impacting, *was my only option. Embracing it as an opportunity, I made a choice to work the situation into the content of my seminar. This, after all, was a seminar on Mastering Conflict.*

Twenty minutes before showtime, my client arrived. She made the choice to **push it away.** *She went into a panic moving chairs* *around in a breathless frenzy. I tried to stop her, but she was so focused on making it right, I could not.*

Later my client thanked me for staying so calm.

**Every significant interaction either diminishes
or increases your energy, influence,
and balance. The choice is yours.**

It was frustrating for both of them. Matt was much more verbal than Ellen. When they disagreed, Matt would immediately speak his point of view; Ellen would half-heartedly agree, not sure how or what she felt. The conversation would end with him feeling resolved and her feeling confused.

Usually by the next day, Ellen would have found some clarity about how she felt and would bring the issue up again. This created a whole new conflict. She continually felt inept with her communication skills in this relationship.

Eventually, Ellen learned that her process was to stand still when she was in conflict. Had she been aware of this, she could have stated in the beginning that she needed a little more time to process how she felt about the issue. There is nothing wrong with that.

Over the years, as Ellen has practiced the concepts in this book, she has more clarity about her views and is better skilled to express those views more quickly.

SET THE LEAD

We often lead in the subtlest way.

In *aikido* practice one person leads by providing the energy, or attack, and the other person responds. How an "attacker" provides energy leads to how a beginner, in particular, responds: Vigorous energy leads to vigorous response. Mean-spirited energy leads to hard, intense response. Weak energy leads to minimal, often ineffectual, response.

Believe me, you learn this quickly when you are physically involved!

I've noticed that the same is true off the mat. For example:

- Habitually beginning meetings late leads to participants arriving late.
- Blaming someone leads to a defensive response.
- Giving unclear direction leads to unclear results.

Not getting the response you want? Check to make sure you are setting a clear lead. A clear lead is behavior that reinforces what you want: beginning a meeting on time regardless of whether every person is there; asking questions to gain clarity about a problem and start a dialogue; being very specific about what you expect from people and checking to make sure they understand.

Now flip the scenario. You are on the receiving end of unclear leads. For example, you come to a meeting on time and the leader doesn't begin. What do you do? Typically, what happens is that the next time the group meets everyone arrives late. The lead was set to begin late.

Using Spiral Impact, you would calmly ask if in the future, the group would commit to beginning on time or possibly change the time to one that works better for everyone.

Returning to the *aikido* context, the advanced *aikido* student responds clearly with sincerity, regardless of the energy or intensity of the attack provided. Off the mat, an advanced student:

- Shows up on time
- Diffuses blame by choosing to learn more about the situation
- Asks for clear expectations

If you find yourself in annoying, unclear situations, ask yourself these two questions:

- Am I providing a clear lead?
- Am I responding to someone else's unclear lead honorably with questions for clarity?

UNDERSTANDING OTHERS (IT)

On the *aikido* mat, momentum is maximized as I connect and blend with my opponent. Blending happens as I move in the same direction as my opponent. In essence, I "gain knowledge" about his intention as I move and look in the same direction. Simultaneously, my movement causes him to lose his balance and become open to my influence. If I attempt to force him in a different direction than his initial intention, he becomes more committed to his position, and we get stuck. While we will focus on everyday interactions here, the same principles apply to things and events.

CONNECT AND BLEND

Consider this situation:

A physician shared that the most frustrating part of his day was going to the lab and telling the lab technician, "I need this sample done by tomorrow." The lab technician's sarcastic response was, "Well, that's too bad."

Of course, the physician had an opinion that the lab tech should do as he said; the lab tech had an opinion that the physician was not his boss. Both people left the interaction not feeling all that great. Perhaps the lab technician felt he had won, but nobody was really winning in this situation, least of all the patient.

The physician had connected with the lab technician, but he had failed to blend. To blend, follow these two simple rules:

1. Turn your statements into acknowledgments, questions, or both
2. Check your physical position

Let's explore both rules.

Rule #1 Turn Your Statements into Acknowledgments, Questions, or Both

"You must be a martial artist because you bow to me when we begin," someone said to me at a meeting. While funny, there is deep lesson to be learned here.

The martial bow is about acknowledging and honoring the interaction, the other person. On the *aikido* mat, the bow is accompanied with asking *Onegaishimasu?* which, translated into English, means, "Will you do me this favor?" I like the bowing ritual and the honor it conveys.

*Acknowledgment creates the proper
space, or container, to engage.*

Each person I engage with throughout my day has his or her own "stuff" going on; many are overwhelmed. Plunging into my agenda before I connect with the other person or people feels like walking into a wall blindfolded...and it doesn't make for great relationships.

Acknowledging the other person's mental and emotional states is important in healthy relationships and even more so in strained relationships.

How do I acknowledge to engage instead of actually bowing?

- Simply ask, "Is this still a good time?"
- Address the person by name and ask a question about something you know is important to him or her.
- Show up on time, prepared and centered.
- Turn off and put away the phone.
- Pay attention to the person or people's energy/body language, then pause and ask a question to bring everyone into the present.
- In a group, ask everyone to weigh in on their current state using a weather analogy (stormy to sunny) or number system. Even better: If time allows, have everyone briefly share a highlight or lowlight going on in their work or life.
- Adjust the physical space so it is comfortable and appropriate for what you plan to do there.

Reflect for a moment: How do *you* personally "bow," or acknowledge, before you engage?

SIMPLE EXAMPLE OF CONNECTING AND BLENDING

*When pulling your car out onto a busy road, what
do you do to get someone to let you in?*

*Next time, if it's not something you already do, try rolling
down your window and making eye contact with a person
in the ongoing traffic. This almost always works. If they
don't want to let you in, they won't look at you.*

*When you just pull out in front of someone with no eye contact,
they usually get mad. Likewise, when someone just pulls out in front
of you without acknowledging you, you probably get mad too.*

So, let's apply all of this to our example with the physician and the lab technician. The physician could start out by acknowledging the lab technician by name and simply asking him, "How are you?" or "It looks like another busy day in the lab." or "I like the way you reorganized the flow of work in here. How's it working for you?" If appropriate, he could also ask about something not-work-related, "How was the baseball game last night?"

But avoid "why" questions because they often create a defensive response. If the physician had asked, "Why, not?" when he was rebuffed, the lab tech most likely would have stressed the impossibility of the request even more.

I ask clients to consider the statements they make about their specific conflict or challenge. In the physician example he may be making statements to himself like:

- "I get no respect."
- "This place is so dysfunctional."
- "If I were in-charge..."
- "I shouldn't have to be dealing with this."

All those statements keep the physician stuck and don't move him toward his "it" of providing quality, timely patient care.

Consider the following prompts:

ACKNOWLEDGMENTS	
Thank you <name> for...	Ouch!
I appreciate...	You did <whatever it was> really well.
Does this time work for you?	It must be frustrating to....
I can see your concerns.	This is <awkward> <amazing> <challenging>

QUESTIONS FOR YOURSELF	
Is this true?	What can I do differently?
What is my part of this?	What if I could...?

INQUIRY QUESTIONS	
Tell me more...?	How did you come to this idea or conclusion?
Help me understand...?	What if, you tried...?
Have you considered...?	What do you think would happen if...?

SPIRAL WITH QUESTIONS FOR BETTER UNDERSTANDING

The concept of asking questions also ensures you know what people mean. Good listening is often not enough. If you move with what you heard (spiral), following it deeper and exploring your assumptions, you learn more. For example:

I listened and heard clearly:

"She is a bully." I thought she must intentionally hurt people. I WAS WRONG. When I spiraled and asked, "What is she doing to earn that reputation?" I learned she is asking people to deliver on commitments.

I listened and heard clearly:

"He is crazy." I thought his behavior must be dangerous to himself or others.

I WAS WRONG AGAIN. When I spiraled and asked, "How do you experience him as crazy?" I learned he is insecure in the relationship and tends to leave when he feels threatened.

I listened and heard clearly:

"People are afraid to tell him what is going on." I thought he must be reactive and scare them.

I WAS WRONG AGAIN. When I spiraled and asked, "What makes them afraid?" I learned people didn't want to overwhelm an already busy person.

When merely listening, my conclusions were based on my own assumptions.

Each time I was wrong!

Another important point: The questions you ask and acknowledgments you make must be sincere. Sincerity is another aspect of nonverbal communication. If your intention is to manipulate, this technique will not work and will often make matters worse.

Returning again to the physician scenario, you might ask, "Why should the doctor have to do all this? Who has time for all this connection stuff?"

Twenty years ago, this situation may have played out very differently, and the technician might have lost his job for being disrespectful to any physician. In the workplace today there is not as much automatic respect accorded to those people with certain titles. People are stressed more than ever and are less likely to blindly cooperate. People are also used to changing jobs and companies more frequently, so there isn't as much fear about upsetting the apple cart.

Here is a different example from the perspective of selling ideas or products:

Martina was beside herself with excitement. She had started a new business selling wellness products. She was convinced these products were the best things out there and she was going to make an enormous income from her venture. She approached people with such righteous enthusiasm, she scared them away.

Disappointed by her lack of success, she revisited the Spiral Impact method. She realized that her sales strategy was causing people to avoid her. The next time she approached a potential customer, she spiraled by asking questions rather than making statements. When she learned about the person's challenges, she'd bring up the products—and then only if appropriate. She found people to be much more receptive; selling was so much easier.

. . . .

Often people are reluctant to engage with people they don't like. The old adage, "Keep your friends close, and your enemies closer" is very true. The closer we are to our enemies, the more we can learn about them. We may learn they are more like us than we assumed. And keeping them close may lead to a positive outcome for both people, as in this example from my own life and work:

When I first started my business, I went to a local professional meeting to network and learn. I crossed paths with a woman from my past. She was a person I did not care to be around.

As a student of my own work, I observed how I wanted to avoid her. I made a conscious decision to make a different choice and be open to connecting with her. She asked if I would like to have a cup of coffee and catch up after the meeting. I agreed.

It was tempting to be thinking judgmental statements about her. Instead, I asked myself, "What makes her successful in her work? What might I learn from her about this new field? How has she changed since I last saw her?" Much to my surprise, I really enjoyed the exchange with her. We went on to do some work together.

> **"If we could look into the secret history**
> **of our enemies, we should find in each**
> **person's life, sorrow and suffering enough**
> **to disarm all hostilities."** –LONGFELLOW

Now, let's move on to:

Rule #2 Check Your Physical Position

Physical positioning is extremely important when meeting someone in person. If you approach him directly, face-to-face, he will tend to be defensive. If you approach him at an angle or side by side, he will innately feel less defensive. Remember the last time you were in an argument or witnessed others arguing? You were likely face-to-face. According to Daniel Goleman in *Emotional Intelligence*, 90% or more of an emotional message is nonverbal. Physical position is just one way to convey a nonverbal message, face-to-face says "I want to control," while an oblique angle says, "I want to understand."

Control   Understanding

FIGURE 8: *Physical Positioning*

Here are ways of using your physical position to improve mutual understanding and continue building momentum between people in conflict:

- Take a walk or a drive for tough conversations
- Sit either next to or at an angle rather than directly across
- Make sure to not sit or stand too close
- Stand at an angle

When a group is meeting, if there are two sides to an issue, the group will typically sit on opposite sides of a conference table. If this happens, it will be difficult to come to an agreement. Arrange the room so everyone is looking in the same direction.

> *"The resolution of conflict is rarely about who is right. It is about the acknowledgment and appreciation of differences."* –THOMAS CRUM

KNOW WHEN THE ENEMY IS YOURSELF

"TURN YOUR STATEMENTS INTO ACKNOWLEDGMENTS, QUESTIONS, OR BOTH," applies to those internal conversations you have with *yourself,* too.

When you feel stuck, you are usually thinking in statements. For example:

- I hate details.
- I'm not good with follow-up.
- I am a loser.
- She isn't listening to me.
- This always happens to me.

Statements are static. They create no movement. When a statement is transformed into a question, movement occurs:

- What are some strategies for dealing with details?
- You are good with follow-up. What is your process that you'd share?
- I wonder what caused him to respond like that?
- Have I listened to her?
- I wonder if I ought to change my approach?

Acknowledgments also create movement.

- I've been here before and things will become clearer with time.
- Everything works out in the end, if it hasn't worked out it must not be the end.
- I have had success before, I know I can get there again.

Go back to Figure: 6 The Vision Path, in Section 2, Knowledge Quadrant, where you wrote down how your situation is blocking you. What is a question you can ask yourself about the situation? Does the question get you moving?

EVEN NICE STATEMENTS CAN KEEP YOU STUCK

It was an ordinary Tuesday. I was between appointments and stopped at Sam's Club to pick up a few things.

When I came out to get in my car, my electric blue Mini Cooper wasn't where I parked it. It's usually easy to spot in a parking lot. As I walked further into the lot, I spotted my Mini next to a minivan and a man with a cell phone to his ear. I quickly realized I had not set my parking brake, and the car had rolled down a slight incline and hit his rear fender.

I walked up, and before I could say anything he stated, "I am a minister. I have a parishioner in the hospital. I don't have time to deal with this."

Startled by his tone, I replied, "I am so sorry. This is obviously my fault. I will take care of it. You're in a hurry; let's exchange information, and you can get on your way."

"Oh, no, we need photographs to document this is your fault," he came back. Neither of us had a photo feature on our cell phone. Looking around, he said, "Maybe we should call the police." I said, "If you'd like to call the police, that's fine. Although I'll give you my insurance company's information. I'm not sure the police will come to a parking lot."

As he called the police, I leaned into my car and put the parking brake on to prevent any further damage.

He hung up his phone and said, "The police won't come," with an air of frustration.

I felt stuck. Nothing I offered seemed to move him to solution. I was even taking full responsibility, and it didn't help.

Then, I remembered to apply what I teach: **Change your statements to acknowledgments, questions, or both.**

I calmly inquired, "Tell me about your parishioner in the hospital." As if I had flipped a switch, his demeanor totally changed. He shared the details of his parishioner's situation. I listened intently.

This moved us to a different space.

He called his insurance agent to ask for advice. I overheard him say, "She seems really nice."

He hung up the phone and suggested he get some quotes on his car and that perhaps we could settle this without insurance companies. I said, "I'd really like that!"

He later admitted to me that when he saw my car, he had made an assumption that it must be some young, irresponsible kid driving the car.

The next day I received a phone call; it was the minister, and he said, "It was so nice to meet you yesterday!"

Do you ever find yourself in a struggle with someone, and all the apologies and explanations get you nowhere?

> **Statements of apology and responsibility got me nowhere. A sincere inquiry acknowledging his stress made all the difference.**

OPEN YOUR EARS—LISTEN

Through the years, I have become less interested in talking and more interested in listening. This is probably odd for a professional speaker and trainer to say. But I find people fascinating.

Choosing to be fascinated rather than outraged places you in a position of power and influence.

Choosing to be fascinated rather than outraged places you in a position of power and influence. When I say "fascinated," I mean "curious." You learn so much by observing and listening. People who interview prospective employees know this well. Sometimes you learn more from how a person fills an extended silent pause than from days of asking specific questions.

When your mouth is open, your ears are shut.
The most obvious situations when it is difficult to open your ears are when you:

- Think you are right
- Are overwhelmed with other things
- Don't like or respect the person talking
- Don't feel respected by the person talking; they don't listen to you either
- Feel attacked and are defending yourself
- Can't follow the person's thoughts because they are not expressed well

The more subtle situations when it is difficult to open your ears are when you:

- Know the topic very well already
- Know someone so well you think you know what they are going to say

The two most important skills to develop to improve your listening skills are:

- Centering (You'll learn more about this in the Focused Energy section.)
- Turning your statements into questions, as discussed in this section

Understanding Groups

In *randori*, the most intense practice in *aikido*, multiple people continually attack you. Just as in any team situation, the dynamics change when a group of individuals comes together for a task. I may know myself and you, but put several of us together, and another dynamic is created.

They were a lively group, mostly young men. Some of them weren't too happy to be in this seminar, Mastering the Art of Conflict, because they believed they already used conflict to gain momentum and inspire innovation.

A couple of dominant players informed me that they intensely argue and debate to innovate. I asked them if they knew whether this worked for all the people on their team.

As they considered the question, a woman's voice filled the silence, "I am one of those people whom this does not work for. I can't stand it when you guys get all intense. I cannot contribute in that environment."

Her sincerity stopped them in their tracks. Their eyes opened wide with surprise. They had never considered the impact of their style on the team. I could tell that several other men in the group agreed with her but were not going to admit it out loud.

Creative tension is a good thing.
It's the degree we take it to that makes it productive or not. The secret to mastering conflict is to understand and honor the different people in the process.

Making assumptions about another's comfort level with the intensity of the conflict is dangerous. People who tend to assume a level of comfort with people they think they know well sometimes find that they really don't know them all that well. Also, many people's comfort level changes when the conversation moves from one-on-one to a group.

Paying very close attention, cultivating awareness, is key to understanding the group. In the Focused Energy Quadrant, you will learn a skill, centering, to help develop awareness.

A WORD ABOUT PERSONALITY/BEHAVIORAL ASSESSMENTS

Just about everyone I've met has at least one person they have real difficulty understanding and relating to. In the past, I didn't like to use assessments as I didn't want to put people in a box. More recently, I have found *Everything DiSC®* extremely helpful. Now, I use it as a regular part of my coaching and team development. While personalities and motivations for behavior are complex, *Everything DiSC®* can explain and simplify our understanding of personalities in a very short period of time. There are many versions of *DiSC®*. I like *Everything DiSC®* by Wiley & Sons Publishing because it is more accurate as they use adapted testing, which drills down more deeply to clarify your answers. Also, the results are in a form that is very user-friendly, more nuanced, and repeatable. Find information at **http://karenvalencic.com/resources** or check the back of this book for more details.

At a 30,000-foot view, DiSC® defines four basic personality styles, of which we all exhibit varying aspects:

- Dominance—motivated by problem-solving, tends to be very direct and action-oriented
- influence—motivated by people, tends to be enthusiastic and collaborative
- Steadiness—motivated by pace, tends to be accommodating and supportive
- Conscientiousness—motivated by precision, tends to follow the rules and values accuracy

As you can imagine, having those different styles on a team is very important, but they also introduce competing agendas. Spiral Impact is a method that helps bring these differences together. Perhaps even this 30,000-foot view has contributed to your knowledge—and even has you thinking!

ACTIVATING THE KNOWLEDGE QUADRANT

1. **HOW ARE YOU CURRENTLY RESPONDING TO THE SITUATION?** Refer to Vision Path in Section 2, Knowledge Quadrant.

2. **WHAT KIND OF LEAD ARE YOU SETTING?** Refer to Set the Lead in Section 2, Knowledge Quadrant.

3. **DO YOU UNDERSTAND THE OTHER PERSON OR PEOPLE?** Describe in detail their intentions regarding the situation. Have you asked them or are you making assumptions?

4. **CHANGE STATEMENTS TO QUESTIONS AND ACKNOWLEDGMENTS,** including self-talk and nice statements.

5. **HAVE YOU ACKNOWLEDGED THE OTHER PERSON OR YOURSELF?** Be specific and sincere.

6. **IF YOU ARE MAKING A DECISION, WHAT DO YOU KNOW FOR SURE?** What are you assuming? What other information do you need? Is there another question to ask? Have you asked, "what if?"

7. **HAVE YOU GIVEN THE KNOWLEDGE TIME TO REST–PERCOLATE?** (See the Focused Energy Quadrant, below.)

8. **CONSIDER** *Everything DiSC® Personality Assessment* for yourself and team. These are available by contacting: **info@ karenvalencic.com.**

THE FOCUSED ENERGY QUADRANT

BEING THE CALM EYE OF THE STORM
Focused Energy, Not Time, is Your Greatest Asset

An eight-hour workday doesn't equal eight hours of work. If someone doesn't feel well or is emotionally distracted, he or she will be lucky to perform productive work for four hours.

While willingly investing resources for employees to obtain knowledge and for executives to plan strategically (intention), businesses oftentimes create situations that diminish employees' focused, vibrant energy. The concepts in this Quadrant address what I believe to be aspects of "human resources" most neglected and underused by businesses today: emotional intelligence, resilience, and the ability to create and maintain personal balance and clarity.

In this Quadrant you'll learn about:

- DEVELOPING CENTER—Becoming the calm eye in the storm: focused, balanced, and intuitive
- REPLENISHING SUPPLY—Charging your body with good fuel through diet and exercise

- **RESTING FOR CLARITY**—Letting your body, your decisions, and your thoughts rest and recharge
- **ACTIVATING THE FOCUSED ENERGY QUADRANT**—Tips for mastering Focused Energy

FOCUSED ENERGY

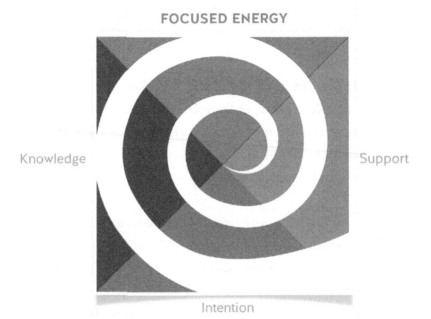

Knowledge

Support

Intention

FIGURE 9: *Spiral Impact Quadrants Emphasis on Focused Energy*

DEVELOPING CENTER

What Is "Centering?"

The calm eye of the storm, the center, is the storm's strength and stability in the surrounding chaos. The process of centering, which I'll describe shortly, is fundamental to *aikido* practice, providing calm strength and stability for powerful and grace-filled movement. Centering is also fundamental to powerful and grace-filled performance in everyday life.

Centering will increase your ability to:

- See all sides of a situation with increased perspective
- Stay calm in intense situations
- Raise your intuition and awareness of others' hidden agendas and feelings
- Stay focused and balanced
- Increase trust by being your authentic self
- Develop your emotional intelligence
- Open your eyes and mind to innovate ideas

Centering is an internal focusing process we do to create a sense of balance, calm, and personal strength. It is our method for becoming the calm eye of the storm in the midst of the activity of our lives. We naturally become centered during certain situations. You have most likely experienced this state at some time in your life.

Times you may have felt centered were when you:

- Were totally engaged in a creative project, such as solving a problem, creating art, or learning something new
- Spent time in nature
- Experienced a profound connection with another person
- Celebrated something wonderful, like a wedding or graduation
- Were performing "in the zone" athletically

When you're feeling "centered" you:

- Feel that anything is possible
- Have expanded awareness of the surrounding environment
- Feel as though time slows down or stands still
- Complete tasks effortlessly
- Feel calm and mentally, emotionally, and spiritually balanced
- Feel "present" or fully aware of what's happening in the moment

Take a few minutes and write down a time when you've felt "centered." Make notes of the details. What was the air like? What sounds did you hear? Who was there? How did your body feel? Did you have a visual picture? For example, I think of walking through Muir Woods by myself among the giant redwood trees. I feel the magnificence of nature, smell the moisture and the soil, and hear the birds and bugs. When I am "there," I feel all the feelings in the list above. I return to these feelings as I imagine being back in the experience.

_____

_____

_____

Not being centered is like being in a large city in the middle of six lanes of traffic. People are honking and yelling. You feel confused, scared and overwhelmed.

Reaching the curb feels closer to being centered; you are less affected by the traffic, and you have a little more perspective. Walking up the stairs of the building away from the street feels even more centered; you are even less affected by the traffic and have even more perspective.

Reaching the top of the building is like feeling rock-solid centered. From there, you are not affected by the traffic at all, and you have all the perspective in the world.

Being centered increases perspective and intuition, which leads to better choices and innovative thought.

The key is learning to become centered in everyday life. It is possible. It is within your reach. It just takes a commitment to practicing some simple techniques consistently.

In my seminars I demonstrate concepts physically. If you can feel it and see it, the concept becomes more real. For the concept of becoming centered, I refer to the center of gravity. The center of gravity is the point of an object around which its weight is evenly balanced. All physical objects have a center of gravity, including you.

Your center of gravity is approximately an inch and a half below your navel. The Japanese call this the *hara*, or "belly." This is our center of power and balance.

To demonstrate becoming centered, I have a volunteer stand, and then I push him gently on the sternum. Inevitably he wobbles. Then I guide him to focus on his own center of gravity, or his "center." I suggest he do this with one or more of the following actions:

- Breathe deeply in through his nose and out through his mouth so he can feel his belly move
- Place his hand on his center point
- Imagine he has eaten an M&M®, and it is in his belly
- Imagine music or movement in his belly
- Notice the feeling of his feet on the ground
- Lift his shoulders to his ears then relax them down

Then, as he focuses on his center, I push on his sternum again. He does not wobble.

Figure 7: **Wobbly**   Figure 8: **Centered**

FIGURE 10: *Wobbly vs. Centered*

All he has done is shift his focus, and it has changed his response to outside pressure.

> *When you are centered it changes*
> *how you interact with everything.*

PRACTICE CENTERING

Students have asked me, "How will I ever get anything done if I am always focusing on my center? How will I be able to have a conversation with someone?" Practicing centering is just like when you begin anything new. When you were learning to drive a car, it required all of your attention. As you became more comfortable, you could do all kinds of things and drive at the same time.

Just as with any skill you want to develop, centering requires daily practice. There are many ways to practice. I encourage you to make it part of your routine and use everyday activities to reinforce it.

Here are some suggestions:
- Begin the morning with breathing and/or meditation. See Section 2, Focused Energy Quadrant about breathing and mediation.
- As you are driving, breathe deeply so you can feel the seat belt press on your center. (Check out Spiral Impact, Strengthen your Focus and Balance, Volume I. This audio recording provides guided practice while you are driving.Get a free download at: **https://karenvalencic.com/resources/**)
- Focus on your center during any physical activity. This is accomplished by initiating your movement from your hips and breathing "into your belly," or from your diaphragm. Centering also improves your performance because it increases your balance and unifies your body movement. For example, great runners look as though they are being pulled by a string from their center; great swimmers shift their hips back and forth as they swim rather than just turning their necks. Golf, baseball, and tennis are all improved by centering. Cutting the grass or pushing a grocery cart or stroller? Move from your center.
- Standing in line? Focus on your center by breathing deeply to feel your belly move.
- Before answering the phone, take a moment to center before you answer.
- While sitting in a meeting, breathe deeply to better listen to what others are saying.
- Take a walk in nature.
- Keep an appreciation journal, make a daily practice to write out what you appreciate, small and large. This shifts your focus to the gifts in your life, which is very centering.

- Engage in the Essential Practice: Misogi breathing and meditation. (See below.)

ESSENTIAL PRACTICE
Breathe for Energy and Relaxation

Breathing is the most essential human intake. You can survive days without drinking or eating, but stop breathing for three minutes, and you die. Breath provides the oxygen the body requires to keep moving. Also, breath is the body's way of eliminating 70 percent of the waste it generates.

Thousands of studies connect our emotional state to our breath. Try this: Breathe quickly in-and-out of your mouth. Do you feel relaxed or anxious? Now, breathe in slowly through your nose so you can feel your belly expand. Then slowly exhale through your mouth. Do you feel relaxed or anxious?

Holding the breath and shallow breathing are the two most common breathing dysfunctions. Daily breathing practice is the best way to improve your breathing habits. I recommend *Misogi* breathing, translated as "mind-body purification." I like this practice because of the movement, which reminds me to keep breathing. Once you find your rhythm you will find your breath moving you. I find it very comforting. I hope you do too.

MISOGI BREATHING

1. **SIT ON A LEVEL-SEATED CHAIR** or kneel on the floor, sitting back onto your heels.

2. **BEGIN BY EXHALING SLOWLY** through your mouth and making an audible noise, "ha."

3. **SIMULTANEOUSLY, MOVE YOUR TORSO** from center forward over your legs at the same rate as your exhale. Keep your back straight.

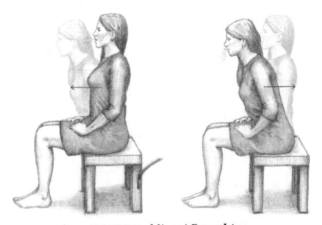

FIGURE 11: *Misogi Breathing*

4. **AFTER YOU HAVE EXPELLED ALL THE AIR** in your lungs, inhale again and switch exhaling through your nose. Simultaneously, move your torso upward from center back to a sitting position.

5. **LET THE BREATH SETTLE.** Repeat when your body feels ready. Slow down if you feel lightheaded.

6. **AS YOU BREATHE OUT,** imagine letting go of anything bothering you; as you breathe in imagine something pleasant coming in.

Try a standing variation by standing with feet shoulder-distance apart, bring your hands together at your chest as if in prayer. As you breathe in raise your hands above your head, then exhale lowering your arms to your sides palms down. Rotate back up to the prayer position and continue to repeat.

When life throws you a big curve such as a divorce, a death, or a health crisis, practicing breathing at least 20 minutes a couple of times a day is of great benefit. Use your imagination to breathe out fear and breathe in love. Or breathe out anger, breathe in peace. When life isn't so intense, practicing breathing will still serve you well; even a couple of minutes makes a big difference.

We have very little control over external events. We do have a choice as to how we respond. Centering and breathing are your best investments to handle any situation with grace.

MEDITATION

Meditation is a life changer. Meditation has been widely documented to have significant health and wellness benefits. While that is a great health insurance policy in itself, consistent meditation also provides you with an orgasmic buzz or hum, and that is pretty awesome too!

Meditation is a life changer.

I've been a meditator for decades. For brief intervals, I have stopped. Inevitably life doesn't flow as well and the noise returns. And I soon restart my practice. Misogi breathing is a wonderful gateway to meditation. For those of us that are "doers," breathing is something you can do. Then, as you finish the deliberate breathing, relax, settle into your center and breathe naturally.

If you find yourself thinking, gently let the thoughts go. Replace thinking with:

- Feeling your breath going in and out of your nose
- Listening to a continuous sound like the HVAC blower, the sound of a river or ocean, crickets—something that doesn't provoke judgment
- Feeling the physical sensations in your body, a spiral from your center that gently sways you, your belly moving in and out with your breath
- Imagine gently loading your thoughts on a cloud to look at later.

15-20 minutes is a good length of time. The benefits of meditation are well worth your investment of time. That hum...is worth it!

FURTHER DEFINE CENTER

We must practice centering because our natural center is at our *hara* (belly), but our operational center is where our focus is, which is typically in our head or heart.

To further explain this concept, consider the following model. There are three different ways we respond to stimuli:

- HEAD (intellect)
- HEART (emotions)
- HARA (center, gut)

When you are in conflict, the cool logic of your head often isn't available. However, your heart's emotions are right there bubbling to the surface. Unfortunately, emotions aren't all that helpful, often causing more problems. In Figure 9, below, the upside-down cones represent the head and heart part of ourselves, and the reason we "wobble" when we feel "pushed."

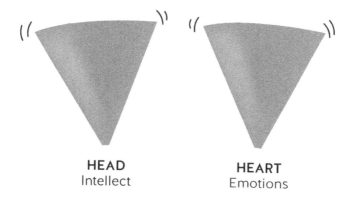

HEAD
Intellect

HEART
Emotions

FIGURE 12: *"Wobbling" Head and Heart*

Notice how there is no stability with either the Head or the Heart. Ever experience two people in an argument, one being overly emotional and the other, overly intellectual? There is no stability there. There is major "wobbling!" The same is true when they are both reacting from their emotions.

Now enter *Hara.*

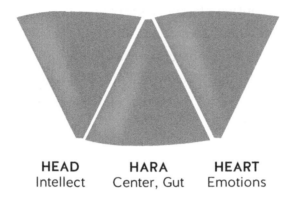

HEAD　　**HARA**　　**HEART**
Intellect　　Center, Gut　　Emotions

FIGURE 13: *Center Stabilizing the Head and Heart*

The *hara*, or center, brings balance to the head and the heart. Notice, it would be impossible to cause the *hara* to wobble. While it is keenly important to develop your intellect by increasing your knowledge and to experience the richness of feeling with emotions, to be a high-performance individual, develop all three aspects of yourself.

Perhaps you have felt conflict within, between your head (intellect) and your heart (emotions)? Your mind says something is a really bad idea, but your heart wants to go for it? In these situations, centering is of particular help. Center yourself by breathing into your belly; imagine each choice as if you've already made it. The best choice will be the one that reinforces your sense of being centered.

Developing center is the single most important
way to bring grace, beauty, and peace to
your life and to those around you.

Centering is the great balancer. If you tend to over-react to conflict situations, centering calms you down. If you tend to retreat or stand still, centering gives you the courage to say or do something you ordinarily might not.

WHEN YOU GIVE AWAY YOUR CENTER

Imagine someone handing you a 25-pound rock. What does it do to your center and muscles? When I work with groups, I will bring a physical rock from my garden and hand it to a leader. People usually look puzzled, but the lessons are vivid.

This represents taking on the weight of another's responsibility or things not aligned with your intent. It will throw your center off and rob others of an opportunity. Because:

> *Strength and talent grow with the weight of*
> *responsibility, just like holding a heavy rock.*

As I work with leaders and teams, this is an important and easy analogy to grasp. Who holds which rock? While collaboration is a beautiful thing, clarity and commitment about responsibility are what moves things forward.

The following are common themes I find in organizations:

Taking on a Rock That Doesn't Belong to You

If someone else has a problem—when do you take the "rock" on and when do you guide him to manage that rock? Many times, the easy short-term solution is to take it on and do it yourself. When you do this, remember three not-so-great results:

- The other person misses the opportunity to develop his or her strength, talent, and knowledge.
- You teach the other person you will solve his or her problems or do their work.
- You may overload yourself with this extra rock.

Identifying Rock Owners

A team meeting is a wonderful thing. People come together to discuss issues collectively. It always surprises me how many times people leave a meeting without clear ownership of next steps. To clarify the rock owners:

- Prior to the meeting, clarify the intent of the gathering.
- At the end of the meeting, ask the question "Who is doing what? And, by when?"
- After the meeting communicate "rock" ownership clearly, in writing.

Collaboration moves teams forward. Sharing the rock and distributing the load are key to engagement and enthusiasm. Be conscious of the distribution and the type of "rock" that suits each person best at his or her development level.

CREATE A CENTERED ENVIRONMENT

Different environments may affect your state of well-being. For example, consider a time you were in a restaurant or a store with loud music and chaotic activity. In the past, just a few minutes in that type of environment caused me to feel off center. By contrast, an environment with soft piano music and lighting, causes me to feel relaxed and focused.

Consider the following for creating a more centered environment for yourself:

- Are there unnecessary distractions? For example, cell phones, computer monitors, television, and clutter all take focus away from the task at hand.
- What do you listen to on the way to work? Does it cause you to feel more or less centered?
- Do you have a plan for your day? Writing down a "to do" list can remove the clutter from your mind.
- How do you eat your meals? Taking the time to sit down for meals is a great centering practice. People have been known to lose weight this way.

As you continue to practice centering, you will become better able to remain centered even in a chaotic environment. Your very presence will affect the environment around you. Do you know people whose mere presence is calming?

You can't change other people.
You can only change yourself.
That is the good news because the only
person you can truly control is you.

GET IT DONE WITH GRACE

Centering is most important on your busiest and most intense days. On the days when your "to do" list is extremely long or you have an intense situation to deal with, you probably tend to jump headfirst into the day.

I find that centering is most crucial on these days. I deliberately center in the morning and throughout the day. Centering expands time. I get more done with less stress when I center. It is not what you do at the end of the day to de-stress that brings peace and grace to your life, it is how you move throughout the day. Consider setting a timer every ninety minutes to take centering break.

Centering
expands
time.

Staying centered throughout the day
increases your balance, influence, and energy,
bringing grace to every interaction.

REPLENISHING SUPPLY

EAT FOR ENERGY

An abundance of raw physical energy is something most everyone wants. Fueling up with good food, oxygen, and exercise gives us energy.

Here are some conclusions I believe are universal. These are not rocket science, they're just back to basics:

- Just like every other interaction, your body's interaction with food either increases or diminishes your influence, energy, and balance. Note how you feel after eating different foods. Not one diet works the same for everyone.
- Eating food closest to its natural form is always best. Processed foods drain the body of energy.
- I find intermittent fasting increases my clarity of mind and energy. Explore the current research. Right now, I find having my last food intake before 6 PM and earliest breakfast after 10 AM works well for me.
- Exercise is a requirement. Schedule it every day just as you would an appointment with your most important client or customer. It can be as simple as a walk or as complex as Pilates. Variety keeps exercise interesting. Find a friend if having company helps you.
- Moderation in all things is a good idea.
- Pure water is the best beverage. Drink at least 64 ounces daily. Drinking it at room temperature is easier on the body because it doesn't constrict your muscles as cold water does.

When it comes to food, I have felt the best in my life when I've viewed food as a source of energy rather than entertainment.

I like to eat colorful food. Most processed food is devoid of color. Vegetables are the most colorful. I stock my refrigerator and freezer weekly with vegetables and lean proteins. Healthy food is easy to prepare. Serving food closest to its natural form requires less effort.

I believe that one of the best investments I can make is in time and good food with my family.

I have always exercised consistently throughout my life. People sometimes tell me I am lucky I do this. But it has nothing to do with luck. Exercising is a choice I make. I schedule it just as I would anything else I consider important. And even though it appears I am taking a break from work, I almost always get my greatest inspirations and ideas when I exercise. Frequently, it is the most productive time of my day.

INFORMATION CONSUMPTION

The amount of information at our fingertips is infinite. Just because it is there doesn't necessarily mean you need to consume it. As with food, pay attention to what information you are taking in. I like to find a balance between being informed without being dragged into drama. Filtering and constantly asking yourself if what you are listening to or reading is adding value to your life is a good idea.

RESTING FOR CLARITY

Slapping or tapping the *aikido* mat is shorthand to your practice partner to STOP, you've had enough. It is wise to know when to stop, sparing yourself injury.

TAKE A BREAK

It is also wise to know when to STOP and rest in daily life. Rest is essential to having enough energy to focus and perform optimally. Research shows that you are more productive when you take a break every 90 to 120 minutes. A break is time to rest your mind or body, or both.

Ideal breaks for me include:

- Leaning back and closing my eyes or, if the place permits, lying down with an eye pillow over my eyes (My favorite eye pillow is silk filled with flaxseed.)
- Getting a drink or snack
- Calling someone who recharges me
- Taking a walk or going outside
- Going out to lunch
- Taking my shoes off and stretching my feet and toes (A tennis ball rolled underfoot is a great massage.)
- Reading something unrelated to what I currently consider work
- Cooking (Yes, for me that is a break.)
- Misogi breathing exercise, as I described earlier in this chapter

What can you add to this list? As I write I am sitting on my backyard deck, and the summer cicadas are singing. Just listening to them for a while is a break for me.

"Mom, what do I do? My cell phone isn't working, and I've got to drive all the way home." I laughed to myself at the seriousness of my daughter's question. Then I calmly assured her that the car would operate just fine (likely better) without her phone.

As a culture we seem almost addicted to being "wired" and accessible. I recently forgot my phone on a three-hour road trip. Initially, I felt anxious to just be driving. Then I made a conscious decision to make it a mini vacation from the world.

It was just me and the road—not even the radio.

The time "unwired" was truly a gift. I had uninterrupted time to think, which generated some creative ideas. My energy was focused by the time I arrived back at my office.

Our wireless technology is a double-edged sword. It makes us accessible to others while often making us unavailable to ourselves and to those physically present.

"For fast acting relief, try slowing down." –LILY TOMLIN

PERCOLATE DECISIONS

The speed of life, aided by technology, frequently pushes us into decisions and commitments before we've really been able let them "percolate." How many times have you left a meeting, replied to an email, or made a purchase, and then had a change of mind? Did you regret it the next day or even the next hour? "Percolation" is letting a decision slowly filter through your values, experience, goals and intuition. Percolation helps you make a clear, unwavering commitment or decision.

Where you locate, or position, yourself is crucial in real estate, martial arts, and life in general. When you percolate decisions, you position yourself ideally to master conflict.

*But remember percolation and procrastination
are close cousins. If you let the coffee
brew too long, it becomes bitter!*

As important as it is to take rest breaks during the workday, it is also essential to unplug for longer periods of time.

*"I've realized that most of my best ideas have
followed a good night's sleep."* –THOMAS EDISON

ACTIVATING THE FOCUSED ENERGY QUADRANT

Rate yourself: How do you feel right now on the following scale?

1   2   3   4   5   6   7   8   9

Centered..Off Balance

Rested .... Tired

Clear, focused..Spacy, edgy

Appreciative .... Fearful

The higher your score the less focused energy you have. Try the following ideas for developing a centering practice.

- Describe in detail how you will practice centering daily.

- How many minutes are you willing to dedicate to breathing and meditation?

- Do you notice feeling spacy or tired after you've eaten? What foods have you consumed? Consider keeping a food/mood diary.

- How will you exercise today?

- If you are feeling angry or frustrated—what is the fear behind your emotion?

- Describe in detail how and when you will take breaks today. Describe in detail how and when you will take a longer, extended break this week.

- Listen to "Spiral Impact: Strengthen your Balance and Focus Audio," free download at **https://karenvalencic.com/resources/**

BEND THOSE KNEES!

THE INTENTION QUADRANT

WHAT DO YOU WANT AND WHY ARE YOU COMMUNICATING?

Many of the best intentions are lost in the wasteland of struggle and stress. Immediate relief from pain and instant gratification intoxicate the brain to reach for the easiest way out. Unfortunately, the easiest way out may have long-term consequences that take us away from our true intentions.

In this Quadrant, you'll learn about:

- DECLARING LEVELS OF INTENTION—Truly supporting achieving your "it"
- THINKING THROUGH INTENT—Pausing before communicating
- CREATING THE PICTURE—Consciously and vividly imagining your ultimate "it"
- QUESTIONING VALUES—Keeping aligned with your intention
- CHOOSING POWER AND GRACE-FILLED LANGUAGE—Choosing words that move you toward your "it"
- ACTIVATING THE INTENTION QUADRANT—Tips for mastering intention

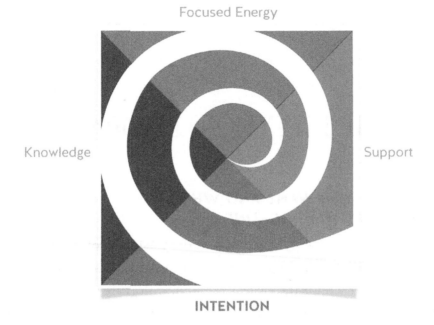

Focused Energy

Knowledge

Support

INTENTION

FIGURE 14: *Spiral Impact Quadrants Emphasis on Intention*

DECLARING LEVELS OF INTENTION

In decades of *aikido* practice, I have seen many people come and go. Some leave and come back, others never return to the practice. But a core group has maintained a life-long intention to practice. For staying power in any endeavor, intention must be lined up at all levels. Defining your desired outcome and declaring your three levels of intention are good places to start.

DEFINE YOUR "IT" OR DESIRED OUTCOME

Webster's defines "intention" in the following two ways that apply to defining what you want out of your endeavor, or your "it":

1. Determination to act in a certain way
2. What one intends to do or bring about

DECLARE YOUR THREE LEVELS OF INTENTION

Most people see intention as something they "set and forget," because they focus on what they intend to do in the moment. However, setting an effective intention is a much richer—and more effective—experience if you declare it on the following three levels:

IMMEDIATE INTENTION: What you want done today or this week. This level includes your "to do" list and specific expectations from others. If your ultimate goal is to build a house, this level would include the short-term activities, for example, interviewing architects and choosing brick.

BIGGER PICTURE INTENTION: What you want longer and broader range. This is the ultimate goal that your immediate intentions pave the path to, for example, having your dream house built.

DEEP PERSONAL (MANTRA OR PURPOSE) INTENTION: What motivates you internally and drives your actions. This level typically reflects your values. Continuing with the house example, you may feel that your deep personal intention is to live comfortably with minimal environmental impact, so you might write that down and refer to it daily, or repeat it as a "mantra," or invocation, before or after meditation to help you keep the intention firmly in mind and action.

Your "It" may be at any level of intention.
But to keep you moving toward your "It,"
each level must support the other levels.

My intentions for *aikido* practice are:

- IMMEDIATE: Commit to practice three times weekly
- BIGGER PICTURE: Demonstrate beautiful *aikido* technique
- DEEP PERSONAL: To honor myself and others in all my interactions

If I supervise other people, my intentions could be:

- IMMEDIATE: To get the task done
- BIGGER PICTURE: Develop my staff to become self-sufficient, creative, and happy employees
- DEEP PERSONAL: Create an environment of healing and love

Back to Section 2, Knowledge Section, Vision Path. Was your "it" an immediate, bigger picture, or deep personal intention? Write your "it" in the appropriate place below. Then define the other two levels that fit with your "it." Refer to the above examples for guidance.

- IMMEDIATE:
- BIGGER PICTURE:
- DEEPER PERSONAL:

Victoria had a very successful medical practice. At one point, she became bored with the tedium of the procedures she performed, bored to the point that she considered a radical change in careers. After losing a lot of money exploring another field in which she had little expertise, investment real estate, she begrudgingly decided to reconsider her medical practice.

Victoria gradually came to realize that she was bored with her work when she focused only on the immediate intention of the day-to-day procedures. As she considered the bigger picture intention of helping people improve their health, she felt more motivated.

Then she discovered her deep personal intention of connecting deeply with the patients who came to her for help, and she found a renewed passion for her work.

Ultimately, her practice grew. Her boredom and burnout disappeared. She truly created a healing environment for all who enter her door.

. . . .

A smile instantly radiated from my entire being. What a pleasant surprise!

On a vacation, my daughter Taylor and I were making our way down a sleepy sidewalk to Starbucks for our morning brew. Suddenly a man broke out in song, serenading us in a beautiful operatic voice.

I don't recall his words, but his intention was clear: to make us smile.

Then he handed us a flyer promoting "cheap tours." He seemed embarrassed.

Then he said, "This job sucks. So, I just focus on making people happy!"

He succeeded.

At times the external world may not match up with your ideal dream. At those times looking at the bigger picture and your deep personal intention—how you can contribute to the world—pulls you through!

David had a very successful career in sales. He opted to retire in his 40s to pursue some other interests. David became a certified personal trainer and traveled to a variety of third-world countries as a volunteer.

David was doing what he loved most: helping people.

About three years into his retirement, a business opportunity was presented to him. A start-up company wanted him to create and lead a sales team. David decided to go for it. He set a time limit for his involvement. He felt good about the decision. It was not a "have to" but a "want to." He also felt it would give him a little more of a cushion financially.

Very ambitious sales goals were in place—the intention was to achieve $10 million in sales by the end of the second year.

After the first year, they were well on their way to meeting their sales goals. However, David was feeling down and unmotivated. David commented to me, "All I'm doing is helping people get rich."

I was surprised to hear David say this because the product was a medical device that prolonged lives. I suggested to David that perhaps he could shift his intention to be one of prolonging life rather than helping people make money. He seemed to be receptive to the idea and went on his way.

I saw David again the following month. He was highly motivated and excited about his work. He said, "I realized that my intention is to bring out the best in everyone I meet." This became his personal mantra, the driving force that got him out of bed every morning. Everyone on his team grew personally and professionally—and they exceeded their sales goals.

When you declare all three levels of intention, you align your daily activities and values to reach your bigger picture intention with power and grace.

THINKING THROUGH INTENT FIRST

When a destructive conflict pops up it's so common to say or think, "That was not my intention."

Intention is one of the most forgotten elements of communication, particularly in sensitive situations.

What would happen if you thought through your intent before you communicated?

Four beautiful possibilities emerge when you think through intent first:

1. **YOU SAY NOTHING.** If you think through what you're trying to accomplish with your communication, you may realize there is not good intent. For example, you may want to "prove" someone wrong, fill quiet space, or complain. I find the more I consider the purpose of my next written or spoken words the more mastery I bring to my communication.

2. **YOU PREPARE THE RECEIVER FOR WHAT'S COMING.** When you begin with your intent it helps you focus your words and the receiver's ears to create context. As mentioned earlier, it's a way of creating the container for communication, as in the martial bow.

3. **YOU BECOME THE MASTER OF YOUR ACTIONS AND WORDS.** Have you ever finished an awkward communication thinking *What happened there?* It used to happen to me quite often. When I begin with my intent, it helps me clarify why what I'm about to say matters.

4. **YOU ANSWER OR UNDERSTAND THE REAL PURPOSE OF THE OTHER.** This applies when someone else is asking or telling you something. Before replying, if you ask them to clarify their intent, or what they need or expect from you, you avoid making assumptions about their needs. For example, *Tell me more about what you are looking for.* Or, *What brings up your question?* Refer back to the Knowledge Quadrant for great inquiry questions.

Reiterating the intent at the end is also a great idea. This concept applies to all communication: email, text, phone, one-on-one and group meetings. Note that you may not always verbalize your intent. For example, if I am sending a text to my daughter, I don't spell out my intention, but I know it is just to connect and let her know she is in my thoughts.

CREATING THE PICTURE

Two common life strategies are "going with the flow" and setting goals. Over the years, I've experimented with both of these strategies and haven't been happy with either in isolation.

I've learned that the best example for living is a river.
A river has a very clear intention of where it is going and at the same time "goes with the flow," altering its course when landslides or other natural phenomena block its path. The river's path is rarely straight, and its beauty comes from its response to ever-changing conditions. It never steers away from its ultimate intention—to reach the lowest point. If the river stops moving toward its intention, it becomes stagnant and smells bad.

For 14 years of practicing *aikido*, I thought, "*Someday* I'll take my black belt test." Finally, I set a goal to take my test. I created a very clear mental picture, or vision, of my test and let it permeate my mind, body, and soul.

Along the way, a knee injury, changes in seminar schedules, and a variety of other issues required that I "go with the flow" and adjust some of the details of how I was going to reach my goal. Many times, doubt about whether I would reach my goal entered my mind, but I'd adjust and stay committed to the goal.

My test would have never happened if I had only "gone with the flow" or only set a goal, especially if I'd rigidly defined how and when I'd reach it.

> *Great accomplishments require clear, deep intention coupled with the ability to adjust.*

Most goals are not accomplished in a straight line, like the "just do it" approach. Accomplishing goals is a process that requires clear intention, increased knowledge, focused energy, and continual support.

Clear intention first requires cultivating a clear vision or picture of what your "It," or desired outcome, is.

My eye shuddered in surprise. It had been poked by a tree branch as I walked through my backyard. I cautiously opened my eye to assess the damage and saw a flash as my contact lens fell to the ground. It was dusk. I needed to go inside to clean the twig debris from my eye (and check for blood!). Finding my contact lens would have to wait until morning.

My contacts are a specialty type and not easily replaced, so over the years I have perfected the secret to always finding a lost lens: keep a clear picture of the lens in my "mind's eye" (no pun intended). If I lose the mental image I have of my contact, I don't find it.

As I fell asleep that night, I pictured my contact in the grass. In the morning it was raining, a cold February rain. I altered my picture of the contact to include the rain. Feeling confident, I took my time enjoying my morning cappuccino before I went outside.

The possible retrieval area was quite large, but it took me only about two minutes to locate the lens!

Create a picture of your "it" in your mind's eye as if it already is happening. You must believe it to be true with every cell in your being. Just a surface thought won't do it. Any minuscule shred of doubt negates it. Committed belief must be present.

When I speak in front of groups, the very same principle holds true. If I have an internal picture of myself giving a great speech and feel it to be true in every cell of my being, I know it will go well. If I have one little shred of doubt, I'm in trouble.

Truly creating vision requires aligning body, mind, and spirit. Every cell in your body has to be aligned and know with no doubt. True, some things are easier for us to align with than others. For example, finding my contact lens is easier than creating a billion-dollar multinational company—but only because of my belief system. While I'm attempting to build a successful business and my mind is setting lofty goals, I may be harboring a hidden insecurity that could be sabotaging success.

Don't take my word for it, though. Experiment.

ENGAGING SOFT EYES

Maintaining focus helps you achieve your intention. But being *too* focused can create blind spots. Another skill from my martial arts study is called "soft eyes" versus "hard eyes." Looking with soft eyes opens your awareness to all that is going on, increasing your breadth of knowledge. Soft eyes are relaxed, opening up a wider area of vision. When your eyes are too focused on only one intent—hard eyes—you miss a lot.

In the example where I discussed recognizing group dynamics, if the two men who thought their arguing sparked creativity had used the soft eyes approach, they'd have noticed the people around them shutting down. In the *randori* example, using soft eyes allows me to see all the people coming at me. If, however, I look at only one person with hard eyes, I'd get clobbered by one of the other attackers before I ever saw her coming.

A personal example: If my hard eyes saw myself exclusively as an engineer, I would have never considered doing the important and fulfilling work I do now. Many inventions come from looking with soft eyes. One that comes to mind is 3M's Post-It® Notes. The adhesive formula was a mistake because it didn't adhere things tightly together. If they hadn't looked with soft eyes past standard requirements, we wouldn't know Post-It notes! The world is full of other examples of mistakes that worked.

There are many examples of how hard-eyes focus can lead to missed information. For example:

- Hard eyes on the bottom line; soft eyes on the importance of retaining talent for accomplishing the long-term vision of the organization
- Hard eyes on getting to work on time; soft eyes to see the new stop sign you just ran
- Hard eyes on an error an employee made; soft eyes on the opportunity for learning and improvement
- Hard eyes on getting married; soft eyes and you may have seen big red flags!

QUESTIONING VALUES

I am frequently asked how to pick a good martial arts *dojo*, which is a place to practice. While I am partial to *aikido*, the most important consideration in making such a choice is the values of the *sensei*, the teacher. When you are putting yourself on a mat and learning a new skill, having values similar to those of your sensei is crucial to maintaining your safety and achieving your purpose for practicing. Similarly, having similar values to those you work with or do business with is important to maintaining your emotional safety and achieving your purpose. Values are the deeper personal level of intention.

Several years ago, I was approaching a rather scary financial transition in my life. Like magic, an opportunity appeared for me to move my business under the umbrella of another organization. I thought, "I love it when life has such perfect synchronization." This seemed almost too good to be true. I discussed this with several astute business friends. All suggested I give it a try, but don't sign any contracts. It took just six weeks for me to realize the arrangement was not for me. We simply did not share values. But the experience was valuable because it reminded me and reinforced my values of integrity and respect, which I had become accustomed to in my other business dealings. The contrast was glaring!

Be clear about what your values are and create a system to check whether your actions and decisions are congruent with your values. Most organizations post their values on a wall, a website and various other places. I find value-based questions more helpful because they cause me to *activate* my values.

ASK THE FOUR QUESTIONS

I ask myself four questions when I engage in a new personal or professional relationship. They are:

- Can I trust you?
- Are you committed to excellence?
- Do you care about and respect me?
- Do we bring out the best in each other?

I've adapted the first three of these questions from those posed by Lou Holtz, the famous former Notre Dame football coach. He and his players agreed that they needed to answer "yes" to each of these questions if they were going to be a team. If the answer was "no" for any one of them, they committed to talking about what was causing the breakdown in relationship. Since they agreed on this ahead of time, it gave them an easier way to bring up and talk about issues. For example, if someone was talking bad about another, it was easy to say, "Hey, we've committed to respecting each other. This isn't respectful."

My colleague, Steve Cambridge, and I added the fourth question. The fourth question gives us more information. I could bring out the best in you, or you could bring out the best in me, but we may not bring out the best in each other.

The second question, "Are you committed to excellence?" requires defining "excellence" in any given situation. First ask yourself, "How do I personally define excellence in this context?"

These questions reflect my values.
What question(s) reflect your values?

These four value questions create a powerful working agreement prior to committing to working together.

I was tasked by a client several years ago to gather vendors for their launch project. My client also requested that I include a current vendor, which they were not happy with already because of their poor service and quality. I solicited bids from two other vendors and the current one. The two new vendors immediately responded. Trusted colleagues recommended these vendors; their behavior during the bidding process also caused me to say "yes" to all four questions. The current vendor was a different story. They took three days to return my initial call. Then, they didn't submit their proposal on time. Finally, their price was significantly higher than the other two. I was surprised when my client chose them for the project. I wasn't surprised at the launch when their part of it failed. Who did that vendor blame? Everyone else.

Honoring those four questions would have provided a better outcome.

Frequently, the people you work with are a given—you can't choose or change them. In those situations, ask the questions from a different perspective. "Do we bring out the best in each other?" becomes "What brings out the best in each of us?"

These questions can be revealing when you're considering using a particular service-provider again or considering re-entering any relationship. You already have experience with the person or organization and likely have answers to the questions. If you answer "no" to any of the four questions based on prior experience, have a conversation to discuss expectations before re-engaging. Even better, discuss the four questions!

People have different needs. Often they don't share their needs unless asked. But if you ask, you may learn that something as simple as reliable instructions for filing a form fulfills a critical need for someone.

When a need is expressed generally, like "feel respected," ask more questions to determine what, specifically, that person needs to feel respected. One person may feel respected when others acknowledge receiving his or her email. Another person may feel overwhelmed by such acknowledgments and resent them as nonessential and intrusive.

If uncovering someone's needs is your goal, asking the right question is also extremely important.

> A swimming club recently sent out a very elaborate survey to determine what they could do to improve its services to keep and add members. The club leadership had all kinds of ideas including adding soccer fields, sports clubs, childcare, baseball fields—none of which were of interest to me. Had they asked the question, "What, if added or changed, would cause you to consider rejoining?" they would have obtained a simple answer: heat the pool.

There is a multitude of applications for the four questions. They are powerful and give you clarity if you take the time to think about them. Making decisions based on the four questions can save you a lot of heartache. As I was teaching a college course, this situation came up:

> Shannan, an intelligent, perky college student, raised her hand and asked, "Do these value questions apply to boyfriends?"

> I responded with, "In your relationship how many of these questions can you answer "yes" to? Can I trust you? Are you committed to excellence? Do you care about and respect me? Do we bring out the best in each other?"

Her eyes widened, she blushed a bit and said, "I have my answer!"

I am amazed how frequently people have a bad experience in a business or personal relationship and give it a second chance without any serious conversation or agreement to do things differently.

> **"Fool me once, shame on you. Fool me**
> **twice shame on me."** –OLD PROVERB

FIND THE TRUTH IN THE FEET

Randori, an *aikido* practice, is when multiple people continuously attack you. Sometimes your attackers use bamboo sticks as weapons. Your task is to maintain center, keep moving, and avoid getting whacked on the head. This practice is challenging and frequently overwhelming—just like life, when too much comes at us at once.

One day randori practice was magical for me. We practiced with our eyes half shut—our focus was on our attacker's feet. I was surprised. *It was easier.*

The key was to watch our opponent's true movement instead of the distracting motions of the arms or sticks. The feet reveal the opponent's intention.

The truth is in the feet.

Extraneous details or comments often throw us off the true movement (or vision) of a project or conversation. For example:

- In the heat of a project with aggressive deadlines, one more change or roadblock can seem insurmountable. The changes and roadblocks are like the sticks in randori! Keep an eye on your actual progress, and your vision will make it easier to continue.
- A too long "to do" list can feel like randori. That's when we need to evaluate each action item to make sure it supports our desired outcome, intention.
- Are you in a frustrating negotiation? Does the other person flip flop and throw curveballs, changing where you thought you were heading? What is at the core of what they want? Continue to bring the discussion back to intention. Keep your vision clearly imprinted on your mind.

When life gets intense and overwhelming, it's always an indicator to get centered and realign with all three levels of your intention. Ask yourself, "Am I using Spiral power, or am I using force to hammer out results?"

Choosing Power and Grace-filled Language

Morihei Ueshiba, the founder of *aikido*, was pure grace on the mat. Minimal movement, powerful results.

In *aikido* practice when the movements are fewer, confident, and concise, there is much more power and grace. Taking haphazard or too many steps minimizes the effectiveness.

The same is true with language. Confident, concise language gets better results. Consider the following:

- I will try to be there at three.
- I hope to complete that someday.
- I kind of think it will work.
- I might look into that.

When you *try, hope, kind of think, or might,* you are leaving room for an out. When someone tells me she will *try* to be there or *hopes* to complete something, she likely won't.

The strongest statements are those expressed with conviction in the present tense:

- You will have the report this Friday.
- I am clear that this is what I will do.
- I am committed to delivering this before schedule.

> *"There is no try. There is only do or not do."* –YODA, STAR WARS

KEEP IT SIMPLE

My father is one of those rare individuals who can both invent something conceptually and build it with his own two hands. He has the awards to validate his accomplishments. His philosophy is, "The best solutions are the simplest." If you try to make something too complex, it will likely fail. This is also true with communication.

Compare:

"You know when we went to the annual meeting and we were at the airport, you said something that kind of bothered me. It's not like it is all that important, but I feel like I need to bring it to your attention. After all, we have said we want to have open and honest communication. This gets really hard for me.... blah, blah blah."

With:

"Understanding your position so we are aligned is important to me. You mentioned your concern about that expense. Can you tell me more about what prompted your concern?"

The first statement is rambling, confusing, and difficult to follow. It contains irrelevant information that muddies the message. The second statement is clear, states intention, and includes a question for clarity, leaving no room for misinterpretation.

"Simplicity is the ultimate sophistication."
−LEONARDO DA VINCI

BE HEARD

Frequently, when people feel as if someone is not listening to them, it's because they are difficult to listen to or they are not connecting with their audience. When language is not organized and clear, listening to it is difficult. Attributes that make people want to listen to you are:

- Tone of voice
- Passion
- Eye contact
- Your own willingness to listen

A great way to practice and learn about how effectively you speak with others is to replay voicemails or audiotape yourself in conversation, with permission from the other person, of course. Be prepared to be organized when you communicate. Be brief, concise, and clear. I find that organizing a message in threes makes it easy for the listener to track what you are saying. Begin by saying, "I have three things. The first is...." This strategy is often called "the magic of three." The "magic of three" also helps you organize and clarify your thoughts.

PRACTICE THE SPECTRUM OF LANGUAGE

Your choice of words can influence people to join with you or alienate people against you.

Consider language in a spectrum. On one end of the spectrum is attack language, on the other end is influential language. The primary difference between the two is that one end *blames*, and the other end *communicates how it impacts me or my group*. In the middle is a blend of the two.

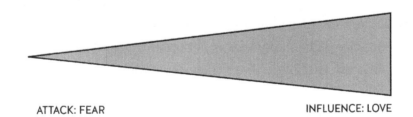

ATTACK: FEAR   INFLUENCE: LOVE

FIGURE 15: *The Spectrum of Language*

ATTACK: FEAR	INFLUENCE: LOVE
Places blame on someone or something else	Expresses how the situation impacts him, her or the group
You always... You never	I am concerned... I feel frustrated...
You never consider my ideas.	It's important to me to be valuable to the organization. I need feedback about my ideas so I can contribute appropriately.
You talk too much.	Thank you for sharing. Now, I'd like to hear from some others on the committee.
You always wait until the last minute.	I feel anxious when I don't have all the information ahead of time. What I need are two days to prepare everything together in the professional way we established.

Attack language often creates a defensive response. Influential language is the best choice if you want to keep momentum going. When you express how a situation impacts you, it can't be debated or countered. However, it is very important not to dilute your communication by being too "nice."

There are a couple of other important considerations before choosing your words:

- Have you connected and blended? Refer to Section 2, Knowledge Quadrant, Acknowledging and asking questions, or both to create connection, gives you more understanding of the other person's perspective and experience. Often, doing this first makes communication much simpler! And, you might even skip this language spectrum!

- What is my relationship with this person? Am I an authority figure, peer, or an equal? Authority figures must set expectations and hold people accountable, which at times may require more direct language. Any of the attack statements listed in the figure above may be stated from center and received without causing a defensive reaction. However, if you are emotionally involved, you may find it difficult to truly be centered, and the statement will backfire.
- What have I tried before? Is this the first time I've communicated about an issue? If I've truly tried influential language and the message is still not understood perhaps it is time to be more direct.
- Refer to Section 4: "Giving Deliberate Feedback" for more suggestions.

I have found influential language consistently furthers cooperation, fosters relationship, and increases influence even in tough circumstances.

And, remember: For best results, always center yourself before communicating!

COME FROM LOVE OR FEAR

Another way of looking at language is to understand that human emotions are rooted in either love or fear. Keeping this in mind can make it easier to choose the appropriate words. I may feel very angry that someone did not call when she said she would. Anger is what I am feeling on the surface, but the root emotion for me may be fear of loss.

Elizabeth Kübler-Ross, MD, and famed author of *On Death and Dying* introduced this idea to me. I've observed this holds true. Kübler-Ross also noted that it is impossible to feel love and fear at the same time because they are opposite emotions. If your intent is to come from love, which is expansive and inclusive, your language reflects so.

Each of the following statements may address the same situation. However, the statements convey very different messages.

- You never call when you say you will. (Conveys fear.)
- I feel angry when commitments are not kept. (Conveys fear.)
- I was worried something happened to you when I didn't hear from you. Please be sure to call next time. (Conveys love.)

CHOOSE YOUR FORM OF DELIVERY

Even in this age of voicemail, email, text messaging, instant messaging, and blogging, the best form of communication for the most difficult issues continues to be voice-to-voice (phone) or face-to-face.

Emails are easily misinterpreted because it's often difficult to convey your mood or intention solely through the written word. Email is great for sharing concrete information, particularly if you want to have a written record. But email can be dangerous for sensitive topics. Recipients inject their own assumptions and fears between the lines. Email is a great way to stay in touch, but for the tough stuff, pick up the phone or, better yet, go for a visit.

Sometimes, with sensitive conversations, we feel we might need either a witness or the emotional support of another person in the room. However, bringing in third parties, even if it's your boss, often amplifies issues. In most situations, begin with the person most directly involved. Which leads us to our next Quadrant: The Support Quadrant.

ACTIVATING THE INTENTION QUADRANT

- What is your desired outcome, your "it?"
- What are the other two corresponding intentions? Be sure they are all consistent and move you toward the same outcome.
- What daily activities are supporting all levels of intention?
- Think though your intent in all your communication before you speak or write and remember the "magic of three."
- Write out your "it" in vivid detail as if it is happening now. Use power and grace language.
- Can you answer yes to the values questions? If not, what is your plan?
  - ‣ Can I trust you?
  - ‣ Are you committed to excellence?
  - ‣ Do you care about and respect me?
  - ‣ Do we bring out the best in each other?
  - ‣ Record yourself talking about your intention. Is your expression clear and concise?
  - ‣ If you feel negative emotion, consider what the fear is underneath the emotion.

THE SUPPORT QUADRANT

SECURING HELP

Support is priceless; indeed, asking for and receiving support may seem like a great expenditure of time and money for some of us. Even supporting ourselves may seem like a great expense. Yet, in the right situation, a third party unfamiliar with a situation can provide such clarity!

In this Quadrant, you'll learn about:
- ASKING PEOPLE—Selecting supportive people to help hold you accountable and talk through issues for clarity
- HAVING THE RIGHT TOOLS—Acquiring the best tools to support you in getting your "it"
- MASTERING TECHNIQUE—Understanding the importance of practicing specific skills
- ACTIVATING THE SUPPORT QUADRANT—Tips for mastering support

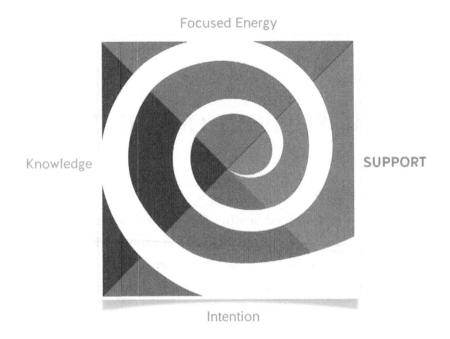

Focused Energy

Knowledge

SUPPORT

Intention

FIGURE 16: *Spiral Impact Quadrants Emphasis on Support*

ASKING PEOPLE

They were relentless. For 40 minutes they pummeled me from all directions with fists and wooden practice knives and swords. At times they were really mean (to give me the opportunity to stay centered in a tough environment). But I kept my composure and responded appropriately to each attack—that was my intention.

Afterward, "Thank you very much," was my somewhat breathless response. My aikido friends had worked me over to help me improve my practice. All challenges help us grow.

As individuals, we can only do so much by ourselves. We are limited by our history, points of view, energy, and self-esteem. Good support is something that not only helps us get to where we want to go, but also stretches us to a level we may never have realized without it.

When I was exploring colleges, I was thinking of studying draft-ing. Later, when I met with the different department heads at my chosen college, they were very supportive and could see something in me I couldn't see in myself. They encouraged me to go for an engineering degree. And they continued to support me throughout my education. I would never have pursued engineering without their support or my openness to receive it.

Personal support comes in many forms, and different circumstances or times in our lives often determine which form—or forms—will be the most effective. You might try one or more of the following sug-gestions, one at a time, or even several over the course of an event or situation.

ENGAGE A MENTOR/COACH/FRIEND

This is an individual you are comfortable talking to and sharing your dreams with. It could be a hired professional or a good friend. I have several friends I seek out as sources of my support. I can call them to bounce ideas around or just drone on about something if I need to. They hear me. Sometimes all I need is to be heard! On a more formal basis, I've hired coaches for specific needs. Whether you enlist friends or hire professionals, be sure to recognize these as support. When you get stuck on a problem, having a resource list of people who can help talk you through it can be the difference between losing momentum or spiraling into success

Sue is an amazingly independent woman. She can do more in a day than five ordinary people. She is also very hard on herself. Perhaps her "opponent" is herself. As I mentioned earlier, sometimes "the enemy is us!"

One day she was lamenting about how frustrated she was with herself. She had set a goal to create a new product and just could not seem to get it done. I suggested we Spiral Impact it. As we worked around the four Quadrants of the Spiral Impact Model, it became clear that she had the knowledge, the focused energy, and the intention. What she lacked was support. So I asked her when I should call her to see her first samples.

She immediately said, "Thursday at noon." I agreed to call her then. Wednesday evening I received a message from Sue, she already had her first samples. She was ecstatic!

Most people, regardless of how independent they are, require support of some kind! In Sue's case, knowing she had support was a great motivation to get her "it" done.

FORM A MASTERMIND GROUP

This is a specific group of people who come together to support and encourage each other. They also provide a sounding board for ideas. Important aspects to creating a Mastermind Group:

- **CHOOSE THE RIGHT PEOPLE.** Mainly, these people enjoy mutual respect and have the required knowledge as well as the willingness to share it with each other. The group can be as small as 2 or as large as 15. But be aware: The larger the group the more difficult the logistics and the longer the meetings.
- **COMMIT TO MEET.** The individuals in this group need to make meeting a priority. Having a consistent group of the same people is important. If the group is local, meeting once a month is usually optimal. If travel is involved, meeting less often is probably more feasible. Note that adding others to the group at random does not work. Building trust is important, and frequently changing members erodes the building of trust.
- **ORGANIZE YOUR MEETINGS.** Each person gets a set length of time for sharing whatever he or she wants help with. An initial meeting might entail getting to know each other by sharing your story, vision-building, or setting goals. Sometimes you may really need the meeting; at other times the meeting may really need you.

Here is a process I've used for facilitating Mastermind Groups, and it works extremely well:

1. Create a flip chart page or a regular size paper with two columns headed "personal" and "professional," then draw a row across for each person. Make sure to leave a little space for notes.
2. Each person rates how they are doing on a scale of 1-10 in both personal and professional life. Make note, if there is something specific you'd like to bring forth for insight from the group. At this point don't go into a lot of detail.

3. After everyone has contributed, one person has their topic explored first. VERY IMPORTANT: The other individuals in the group are to only ask questions about the situation or topic. No advice-giving. No telling a similar story. No changing topic. Ask questions until you can't possibly ask any more. This is true Spiral Impact form!

4. Then ask the person what awareness they've gained. What might they initiate after this conversation? Write that down on the paper. Again, avoid giving advice.

5. Each person then takes a turn.

6. Save the paper until the next time you meet; follow the same process next time you meet and report in on your progress.

> *"A problem shared decreases by half.*
> *A problem held in silence doubles."*
> **–SOURCE UNKNOWN**

JOURNAL

Journaling, writing things down and essentially "talking" through them with yourself, is an easy way to support yourself. Great clarity can come from writing. Sometimes just writing something down helps you let go of it.

I journal to affirm my dreams.

Over the years I have changed how I journal. I used to journal only when I was struggling. Journaling then helped me process whatever issue I was grappling with and let it go. Now I journal to affirm my dreams. I find that if I take time to write down my plans or dreams for the day, life tends to go more smoothly. Often on Sunday evenings, I write down my vision for the week.

READ BOOKS AND LISTEN TO PODCASTS

I love reading and listening to others who add to my knowledge base of self-development and support my ability to stay centered. Since the first edition of this book, YouTube and podcasts have grown to offer an infinite supply of stimulating speakers on research, ideas, and entertainment. TedTalks are a wonderful beginning point that often leads me explore topics more deeply. I find the support of others stimulates my innovative writing and speaking! I'll listen while I drive and forgo the news. Every year I enjoy learning about different people's reading lists. It is wonderful how easy it is to access other peoples' innovative ideas.

> *"We all need someone who will make us do what we ought to do. If you have a powerful conscience, that will function as the "other." For the rest of us, what's required is to surround ourselves with the kind of people who will not let us default ourselves, who will make it necessary for us to do what we have to do in order to pursue our cause in life."* –LEE THAYER, "LEADERSHIP"

HAVING THE RIGHT TOOLS

Falling down and getting up again is another principle fundamental to *aikido*. Having good mats to fall onto is hugely important. For a few years, I practiced with no mats, taking falls on carpet-covered cement. While my falls were perfected to minimize the pain, my back, unfortunately, created its own mat. A firm mat, not too soft and not too hard, is a tool essential for effective *aikido* practice and the long-term health of the practitioner's body.

Do you have the correct tools for whatever you are doing? The right software program can save a tremendous amount of time. A worn-out screwdriver can make the simplest task huge. My smartphone revolutionized my life. Having the right tools makes anything easier.

Draining water from my greenhouse's water tank is a yearly task. Always up for a good challenge, I typically used a cut-off hose to create a siphon. This took a bit of finagling, but when the water finally flowed, I felt the thrill of accomplishment.

Over the years, I found myself beginning to avoid the task; the thrill was gone. It took too much time and the water was gross. Then I purchased a small pump. Wow! All I had to do was sink the pump into the tank and turn it on! How easy. I felt equally or even more thrilled with my new accomplishment. Having the right tool is all it took.

MASTERING TECHNIQUE

A master becomes a master by practicing specific techniques over and over and over again. In *aikido* practice, very specific responses to very specific attacks are repeated thousands of times. Eventually, when randomly attacked, you respond in the most appropriate way without a thought. It becomes natural and part of who you are. You support yourself and others, simply by mastering the technique.

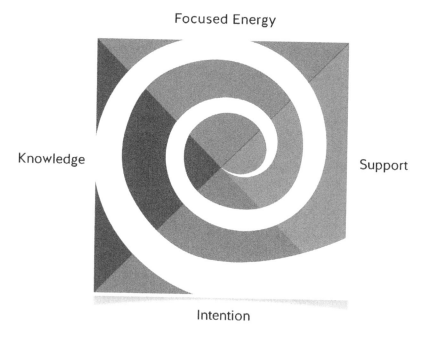

Focused Energy

Knowledge

Support

Intention

FIGURE 17: *Spiral Impact Quadrants*

The quadrants in the Spiral Impact methodology all have specific techniques to master. Each one, when mastered, moves you into graceful action. When you've mastered all the techniques, you have the power to get your "it" done with grace.

MASTER STATING YOUR INTENTION

Know your three levels of intention, as we explored in the previous section. What is your immediate intention, your bigger picture, and your deep personal intention? Also, practice pausing before you communicate to reflect about your intention. You can refer to Activating Intention in Section 2 for more tips on mastering intention.

I met a good friend for lunch. This is someone I don't see very often and value our time together greatly. As we were catching up, an overbearing acquaintance of ours walked into the restaurant.

As he reached over to pull out a chair to join us, time stood still. I knew that if he actually sat down, we would be subjected to his talking at us throughout our lunch.

In that moment I centered myself and stated my intention, "Oh, if you'd excuse us, it is important to me to finish my conversation with Betty. "

He was a little surprised but went on his way. How liberating to be able to state the truth of our needs and get what we want! Knowing your intention and stating it from your center is frequently an easy way of communicating to get your "it." In this case, I knew and expressed my immediate intention, and I expressed it with my deep personal intention, which is about honoring myself and others.

Occasionally, participants in my seminars think that stating the truth of our needs, as in the above story, is being mean. My question then to them is, "Is it mean to be authentic to a rude person?"

This scenario is played out frequently in organizations. One person wants to chitchat with another person who prefers to work. If you're that second person, state your intention. "I need to get this work done right now; can we talk another time?"

Stating your intention can resolve a lot of different issues, but many people find it difficult to do. I believe these people are confusing being nice with being sincere. Being nice oftentimes requires a lie. Telling someone who is obviously ill, "you look great today" is nice. Telling her "it's great to have you with us today" is sincere. Being sincere is honesty tempered with kindness, as in the "I need to get work done" example, above.

> *The goal is not to be nice; it is to be sincere.*
> *Being nice often requires a spoken or unspoken lie.*
> *Sincerity is honesty tempered with kindness.*

MASTER ACQUIRING KNOWLEDGE

So often we think we know about others and come to conclusions based on assumptions and rumor. Master turning your statements into questions and acknowledgments for greater understanding. These statements can be verbalized out loud or remain as thoughts in your head. Also refer to Activating Knowledge in Section 2 for more tips on mastering knowledge.

You could have cut the tension in the room with a knife. A recent merger between two very different corporate cultures had every-one on edge. To make things even more challenging, the majority of the people in the room were introverts. It was a tough audi-ence to engage.

At a turning point, one woman angrily shared, "We are being asked to cut back on expenses, yet they spend thousands of dol-lars repainting airplanes with the new logo." I could tell this was an important issue for this group of people. Notice: The woman said this as a statement. When turned into a question, it becomes, "What was the motivation to change all the airplane logos when money is so tight?"

The answer was that it is a federal regulation to repaint airplanes after so many hours of flying. What appeared to be a waste was actually a necessary expense. How would one know except to ask?

Often I know more of the back story of difficult situations. When I hear what conclusions people make about decisions made without knowing the facts—it is truly fascinating. And almost always wrong. Assumptions are dangerous.

MASTER FOCUSING YOUR ENERGY

Many conflicts in my life have been resolved by getting centered. Centering allows me to have a perspective I don't have when I am not centered. It therefore enables me to be open to learning and less likely to accelerate the tension. See Activating Focused Energy in Section 2 for tips on mastering focusing energy.

I felt outraged. How could someone be so heartless and mean as to share his opinion with another person about something so private in my life? And his opinion had taken the form of criticism! My reaction was to call him immediately. He needed to butt out of my life!

I was in a rage. Fortunately, I caught myself, and I spent time attempting to regain my sense of center. I went to work out at the gym and then sat down to do some deep breathing. Only then was I able to call him, ask a constructive question, and begin a dialogue. I calmly asked," I'm curious about your expectations for our working relationship; what's important to you?" He immediately said, "I know why you're asking this, and I have to say I'm sorry. The minute those words came out of my mouth, I knew I was wrong."

I learned that while his behavior was still inappropriate in my view, his intention was by no means evil.

Had I reacted in a rage, I would have made the situation worse and possibly even given the person in the story justification for his criticism of me. The situation also taught me to be more careful about what I share with whom.

ACTIVATING THE SUPPORT QUADRANT

- Sign-up for my monthly 'Ahh...Yes!' updates at **https:// karenvalencic.com/resources/**; consider receiving bi-weekly "Spiral Questions" also available to sign-up for on my website.

- Make a list of people who can personally support you. Call them. Plan a regular time to connect with them.

- What books and podcasts are you engaging with now to help support you?

- What tools are causing you to struggle and lose time? What can you do to update or replace them?

- What are you doing to master each quadrant? Revisit each activation page in Section 2 for ideas.

  ‣ Knowledge
  ‣ Focused Energy
  ‣ Intention
  ‣ Support

- Check **http://karenvalencic.com/resources** for support updates.

SPIRAL IMPACT
IN ACTION

SPIRAL IMPACT IN ACTION

Moving or entering into an attack is an essential element of *aikido*. Otherwise, you are just avoiding it, going in circles, and there is no impact, much less a desired outcome.

In life, you must enter into and activate each Quadrant to create an impact. As you shift from Quadrant to Quadrant power is generated to make your impact with grace. This is called "Quadrant Shifting." Remember a spiral without direction is just a circle. Going in circles gets you nowhere.

In this section you will learn about applying Spiral Impact to:

- Mastering the Art of Conflict
- Making Solid Decisions
- Getting "It" Done with Grace
- Minimizing Burnout

MASTERING THE ART OF CONFLICT

As a novice attempts to duplicate *aikido* technique, he almost always tries to force his opponent to the ground. Although this is an impact, it lacks grace and requires too much energy. Forcing the opponent is not *aikido*. Blending, connecting and moving with the opponent so she falls or moves easily is *aikido*.

Likewise, forcing an artificial end to a conflict kills creativity and frequently destroys relationships. As Spiral Impact is applied to conflict, it opens the door to all types of solutions.

KNOW WHEN YOU ARE IN CONFLICT

First, you've got to know there is a conflict. When I ask in my workshops, "How do you know when you are in a conflict?" participant responses typically include:

- Increased heart rate
- Tension in the stomach, neck, or head
- Disagreement, which stops progress
- Feelings of struggle or confusion
- A situation different from what you desire

When I feel I am pushing against something, that's my clue I am in conflict, as we discussed in Section One. I can experience this "pushing against" internally or externally. And the person I'm feeling conflict with may or may not be feeling the conflict. It is still conflict.

Another aspect of working with conflict is knowing when someone is experiencing conflict with you. This requires developing awareness, which comes from centering and asking questions. This awareness is particularly important when:

- You are an authority figure
- The other person is unwilling or unable to let you know he or she has a conflict with you

The skill of asking questions you learned in the Knowledge Quadrant and the awareness you developed in the Focused Energy Quadrant are essential tools for increasing your knowledge about the people around you. Only if you know something is wrong can you do something about it. Paying attention and acting on this awareness will help prevent abrupt reactions, which can be destructive to both your personal life and business interactions.

MASTER CONFLICT MAP

To resolve conflict, use the following map.

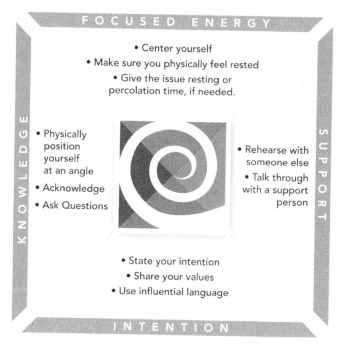

FIGURE 18: *Master Conflict Map"*

For more specific detail about each Quadrant, revisit Section 2: The Spiral Impact Method.

I suggest beginning at the top of the Map, with the Focused Energy Quadrant, when you find yourself in conflict. This Quadrant puts you in a calm state, with the broadest perspective, helping you to make wise choices and keeping you from overreacting.

Then, depending on the situation, I suggest Quadrant Shifting to Intention or Knowledge.

Andy was fuming. He received an email on his phone from his boss. His boss was always so critical and questioned everything he did. Andy had spent days preparing a proposal. His boss hadn't read it but was already questioning it.

Feeling a "push against" his boss, Andy recognized an opportunity to apply Spiral Impact to his conflict. First, he tried centering. But he quickly realized he was exhausted from having been up all night with a head cold. This awareness helped him to also realize that anything he was feeling should not be taken too seriously. His perspective was skewed. It was late in the day, so he decided to let it go until morning.

In the morning, he re-read the email. He then realized that his boss had merely asked a question for clarity about the proposal. It wasn't criticism at all! Later his boss even complimented him on his efforts.

The Focused Energy Quadrant helped Andy to resolve his conflict. First, he tried centering. Then he realized he wasn't physically at his best, so he gave the issue time to percolate and returned to it in the morning with a new, more productive perspective.

Clare shared office space with one other person. They were harmonious office companions. As the business expanded, a third person, Roger, came in to share the space.

It was apparent from the first hour that this was going to be a challenge. Roger talked extremely loudly, particularly when he was on the phone. If Clare was on the phone at the same time, she literally could not hear her caller. Clare felt herself "pushing against" Roger. She decided to Spiral Impact the situation.

She first made sure she was feeling centered. She then shared her intention with Roger: "I really need clear communication with my clients and my co-workers." Then she added in influential language, "and I am having difficulty hearing when we are on the phone at the same time. Could you possibly lower your voice?"

Clare was rather taken aback by his response. "It took me fifteen years to develop this voice, and I won't be changing it." That was the end of the conversation.

Recognizing that the Spiral Impact is a process, Clare realized she needed to Quadrant Shift. She first needed to verify that this was a real issue and not just an overreaction on her part. To gain knowledge, she tactfully asked around and learned that even the office manager, 30 feet down the hall, was having the same issue with Roger's telephone voice.

The next day at a regular staff meeting, Clare brought up the issue. "Roger and I have already discussed this, and I need to bring it up with the group. I really need clear communication with my clients and my co-workers, and I'm having difficulty hearing when Roger and I are on the phone at the same time. This situation is not working for me. What suggestions can the group offer to make this a winning situation for all of us?" Several of the others openly *agreed that this was a problem for them, too. Yet Roger dug in, "This is how I am, and I will not be changing."*

The group froze, not sure what to do about the conflict. Clare had a client meeting, so she had to leave. As she left, the owner of the company followed her out. He thanked her for bringing up the issue and apologized for Roger's behavior.

Roger never did admit that there was anything wrong with his behavior. But he did lower his voice. That was what was important.

This scenario began with Focused Energy and moved through Intention, Knowledge, and Support, with Clare continually checking to make sure she was feeling centered along the way. Note: Clare was wise to try to address the issue directly with Roger first because it gave him an opportunity to help solve the problem without feeling attacked.

Here is another situation.

Their meetings were energetic and fun. They were a great group of people charged with an imaginative task: creating an online presence for the organization. Bill was the team leader.

The only problem was that month after month, one key player had not delivered on what he had promised. He was the designer. He'd have all kinds of great ideas, yet each meeting produced nothing except more great ideas.

Bill realized the need to get the project moving, and doing so would require having a tough conversation with the designer. He Quadrant Shifted around the Spiral. The conversation went like this:

"Dan, I love all the creative ideas you've presented for the website. You are a great asset to the team (acknowledgment). But I am frustrated and worried that the site is not up yet (intention expressed influentially). What I need from you is a hard date for completion." Then Bill just listened for the answer. Dan shared that his workload was such that he could not make a commitment. Dan suggested he pull in someone else to replace him.

Bill was grateful for the honest answer. He brought in another designer and had the site up the following week.

And then there are family situations.
Teenagers are possibly the best teachers for their parents when it comes to mastering conflict. Their passion and energy are a double-edged sword. On one hand, you want your kids to engage with life; on the other hand, you want them safe!

Once, in the heat of a battle with my older daughter, it occurred to me that I wasn't practicing anything I teach! We were definitely both fully engaged in the battle, a disagreement about curfew, and both of us were pushing against each other verbally.

I realized this and I stopped. I centered myself and changed my statements into questions and acknowledgments. I asked her what she thought was fair in the situation. She explained, and I listened.

I acknowledged how frustrating it was to feel controlled by a parent. I shared my intention of getting good sleep at night while knowing she was safe.

When I truly listened to her and acknowledged her, it was like flipping a switch. We began to hear each other, and the emotions calmed down. We moved on to solutions. We created a plan that met both our needs. The plan honored an earlier curfew during the week and gave her more leeway on weekends as long as I knew specifically before 11 p.m. what her plans were. We both followed through on our agreements.

Eventually, the trust level between my daughter and me grew because we listened to and respected each other. I could fall asleep before she came home because I knew I could trust her to communicate and make smart choices. Text messaging became a great way for her to communicate with me without waking me up. If I did wake up, I had a message from her and knew she was okay.

In this situation, recognizing I was in conflict was the first productive step. I stopped when I realized I was pushing. Then I sought Knowledge, changing my statements into questions and acknowledgments. I listened and shared my Intentions. Focusing Energy was a key component throughout the entire conversation.

In the above scenario, I initially reacted out of my fear of losing control of my daughter. Moving into love, I realized that my intention for her was to be a self-sufficient, trustworthy adult. This required having conversations rather than issuing orders. Now she shares almost everything with me, which has strengthened our relationship —but can also be overwhelming!

"Moderate your desire of victory over your adversary and be pleased with the one over yourself." –BENJAMIN FRANKLIN

SPIRALING BACKWARDS

I've noticed over the years in my *aikido* practice that I tend to go three steps forward and then one step back. I learn and apply, learn and apply. Then all of a sudden, it seems I don't know a thing. This has happened to me when dealing with conflict as well. Once in a while, I do everything "wrong."

What I've learned is that this is normal, and I can usually remedy the situation by simply acknowledging that I messed up. It sounds something like this:

- "I don't like how I handled my part of this situation. Can we start over?"
- I've never had anyone say, "No." Often it opens a bigger door toward a good resolution.

MASTER INNER CONFLICT

Internal conflict can be just as challenging, or even more so, as a conflict with another person. Quadrant Shifting around the Spiral can help clear up internal conflict, too.

Two prevalent types of internal conflict are due to either insecurity or indecision. Decision-making is covered in the next section. Let's consider a couple of insecurity scenarios here.

First, when circumstances in life are out of your control, as in Jake's situation:

Business was down, there was talk of a buyout, and rumors were flying about layoffs at Jake's place of employment. Jake felt a lot of internal conflict since he was the sole supporter of a young family. Unsure of where to turn, Jake turned to Quadrant Shifting on the Spiral.

In the past, he would have started drinking more beer, watching more TV, and ignore the situation. He decided to make a different choice and make the situation an opportunity for personal development (Spiral Impact it).

Jake decided first to get a grip on his Focused Energy Quadrant. He committed to beginning and ending the day with breathing exercises. Sometimes he got up early to sit and breathe, other times he did his breathing in the car with his Spiral Impact audio-guided centering. He also decided he'd limit himself to one beer a day because he knew he needed all the Focus and Energy he could get. His wife helped support him in his commitment. This by itself helped him tremendously.

Quadrant Shifting, he decided to combine Support and Intention. He enrolled in a local seminar about career management and transition. He found the other participants and the teacher incredibly supportive. He took a variety of tests that helped him identify his personal strengths and interests. Much to his surprise, his current position wasn't aligned at all with his strengths.

Meanwhile, he continued his breathing and centering practice. Then he Quadrant Shifted to Knowledge. He already had gained a lot of knowledge about himself through the class he took. Now he wanted to increase his knowledge about other possibilities. He made appointments to meet with people in other industries and other departments in his company that he might want to consider as possibilities.

Many people at the company Jake worked for were stuck in fear about what might happen. Jake "kept moving and bent his knees." His internal conflict was gone. Now he was actively interested in exploring where his life would turn next. He recognized that working through his internal conflict was an on-going process. It was important to continue to Quadrant Shift to keep the momentum going and the fear at bay.

Jake ended up staying at his company but moved into sales! The Spiral Impact process helped him realize he really loved working more with people than sitting behind a microscope in the lab. He is very happy and successful today!

Now here is a story about a different type of inner conflict brought on by insecurity.

Heart racing, palms sweating, I felt as if I would pass out every time. Standing up and delivering a presentation woke up every cell of insecurity in my being. I tried all the little tricks. Back then, overhead projectors were the media, and I'd be sure to dim the lights so nobody could really see me.

Needless to say, when I decided to start a business that required public speaking, those close to me thought I was crazy. What did it take to push me through my insecurity? It took passion to share something I felt was extremely important. I was crystal clear and driven by my vision.

Centering was the skill that gave me the courage to stand up and deliver my talks without passing out. I had knowledge to share, and I used the skill of blending to connect with my audience: I asked them questions. Asking questions caused me to relax because at that moment, I wasn't speaking at the group as an authority figure. We were simply having a conversation. My support, ironically, was from my biggest fear: my audience. Their feedback was essential for me to grow more secure.

Did I outgrow the fear each time I present? No. But now I know that nervous fear is essential for me to be "on." When I don't have the nervous energy, my presenting style tends to go flat.

INCREASE THE SPEED OF RESOLUTION

How quickly we resolve conflict and make decisions can be directly related to how clear we are about the Spiral Impact process and how developed we are in each Quadrant around the Spiral. Want to resolve conflict or make decisions more quickly? Master each Quadrant around the spiral.

Remember, though, that if the conflict is with another person, that person likely resolves conflict at a different pace from you. This requires understanding and patience for both people! The ultimate speed of resolution is that of the person who resolves it for him- or herself the most slowly.

MAKING SOLID DECISIONS

Making a decision, or choice, can feel like a conflict when you don't have all the information (or a crystal ball). A decision made in haste can create future conflict.

The Spiral Impact model makes for a good decision-making tool. As you Quadrant Shift, be sure to travel around the entire Spiral. I find sometimes we rush to decisions that often would be better if left to percolate a little bit more. Of course, that depends on the type of decision. If you don't have a clear YES after looking at the map below, most often the answer is a NO or "not now."

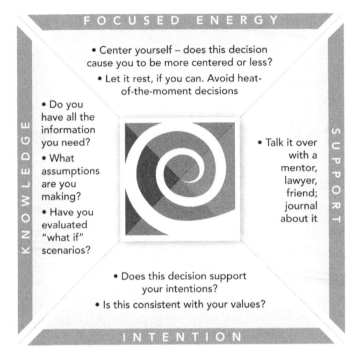

FIGURE 19: *Decision-Making Map*

My daughter and I took a short trip to Sedona, Arizona. When we arrived, we learned a tough lesson about the pitfalls of booking reservations online and were left without a room for the night.

We were lucky to ultimately find a place to stay, though it was in a creepy, old hotel too close to the road. The next day we passed a sign that read, "Ask us about a 2-night stay for free." So we asked. You probably know the story: We were required to listen to a timeshare presentation. I decided to go and listen. Anything to move from the dive we were staying in. And —who knew? —I might learn something.

I was surprised by what a cool program this resort had and became very interested. And, of course, the opportunity was for "this day only" and these places were "selling out quickly." I knew my history; I could be a little impulsive. So I told the salesperson I needed to have lunch and think it through.

When I got out of the heat of the sale, I Quadrant Shifted. Focused Energy was my first stop. I needed to eat because my blood sugar was crashing. Then, as I centered myself, I realized that purchasing a timeshare was not something that brought me more peace; it brought me more stress. Then I shifted to Intention. When I thought about my intentions for the year, they included reducing debt. Buying a timeshare would increase my debt. I had a clear answer: This was not the right time for me to purchase a timeshare.

I went back to tell the salesperson. He thought I was crazy for bypassing the opportunity. I knew I wasn't.

Twelve years later, I have an example of not applying Spiral Impact and making a regrettable decision: I purchased a timeshare. I followed nothing that I teach! It was a weak moment. I'd love to give it away, any takers?

GETTING "IT" DONE WITH GRACE

It was a hot, sticky summer evening on the aikido mat. I had a couple of practice rounds during which I felt very much in the flow. My attacker came at me with a punch. I gracefully moved in a spiral motion, and he could do nothing but fall to the floor. The spiral made the impact easy. A deeper meaning to "keep moving and bend your knees" occurred to me at that moment. That precise moment of contact was when the concept of Spiral Impact was born. I realized at that moment, that most people want to have an impact, or be influential in the world but certainly don't want to struggle.

LEARN PERSEVERANCE

Perseverance is what separates the people who can complete a project or stay with a long-term goal from those who cannot. I believe perseverance is a learned trait.

The archetypical vision of a person with perseverance is one who fights through every circumstance until achieving his or her desired outcome. The truth is that even people perceived to have perseverance get stuck; they have bad days. But they know this and accept it as part of the process. They don't let a few bad days or criticisms stop them.

The Spiral Impact method is a perfect model for learning perseverance. When you do have a bad day or feel stuck, Quadrant Shift! The following is a map with suggestions to support you in your Quadrant Shifting.

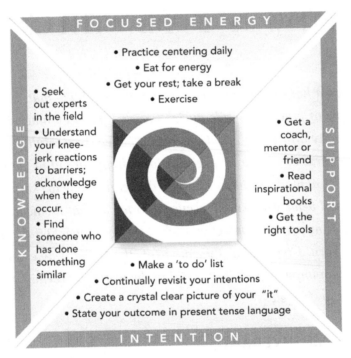

FIGURE 20: *Get "It" Done with Grace Map*

Several times through the process of writing this book, I felt like throwing it out the window! This is when I'd Quadrant Shift. The following are the specific things I did:

Focused Energy
- I'd exercise, meditate, or practice *aikido*. My best ideas for this book always came to me when I was on the mat.
- I'd let the book rest for periods of time and return with fresh eyes.

Knowledge
- I'd seek out other authors and learn about their experiences with writing.
- I'd catch myself before I'd utter, "I am not a detail person," and ask myself instead, "How can I manage the enormous amount of detail this book requires?"
- I'd ask other experts in my field for feedback on my content.

Intention
- I'd commit to writing at certain times during the week. I planned my "to do" list to include specific tasks related to the book.
- I continually revisited and revised all levels of my intention. My big picture intention is to help people live more easily in their lives and work together more collaboratively. This book is an integral piece of my plan to do this. To throw out the book would be to give up a big part of my plan.
- I made sure my writing was consistent with my values.

Support
- I created a list of people I called when I needed encouragement.
- I invested in a laptop (a tool) so I could take my writing anywhere.
- I hired a fabulous editor and illustrator.

MINIMIZING BURNOUT

Many people consider being "really busy" and "stressed out" badges of honor today. This frenzy is fed by demands to get more done better with less time and fewer resources. Unfortunately, these demands can lead to mistakes, costing time, money, and relationships. Over time these frenzied demands can also cause burnout and paralysis. Quadrant Shifting definitely helps to minimize burnout.

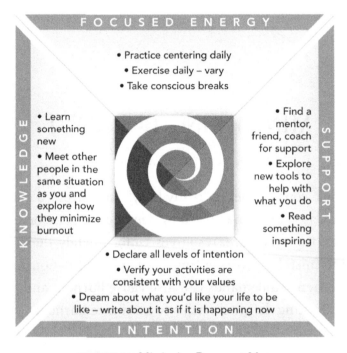

FOCUSED ENERGY
- Practice centering daily
- Exercise daily – vary
- Take conscious breaks

KNOWLEDGE
- Learn something new
- Meet other people in the same situation as you and explore how they minimize burnout

SUPPORT
- Find a mentor, friend, coach for support
- Explore new tools to help with what you do
- Read something inspiring

INTENTION
- Declare all levels of intention
- Verify your activities are consistent with your values
- Dream about what you'd like your life to be like – write about it as if it is happening now

FIGURE 21: *Minimize Burnout Map*

It seemed every day was the same for Maxine. She'd get up, go to work, come home, eat dinner, go to bed, and then get up the following morning and do it all over again. Then the weekend came, which she spent catching up on chores and planning meals for the week. She felt as if she was going in circles.

Maxine was a nurse. She went into nursing because she wanted to care for people. Unfortunately, a shortage of staff caused her to feel overworked. She became cynical about healthcare.

This is about the time Maxine found herself in one of my sessions. When she learned the concept of centering, she realized how disconnected from herself she felt throughout the day. Normally rushing from one thing to the next, she felt numb to the reality around her.

She made a choice to experiment with centering. Every morning she practiced breathing. On the way to work, she'd listen to the Spiral Impact centering audio. She found that as she stayed centered, she could accomplish much more and yet feel calm in the process. She made the time with patients a "centering practice." Every time she entered a room she would breathe deeply and truly be present with the patient. Ultimately, she felt reconnected with her original intention of becoming a nurse.

Then Maxine revisited her levels of intention. She knew her Deeper Purpose Intention was to care for people. She also knew she needed to take care of herself to be able to care for others. She needed support. She found several co-workers who shared the same mindset. They decided to form a reading group. They read inspirational literature together and met a couple of times a week over lunch to discuss their reading. Maxine came to really look forward to the sharing.

Shifting to the Knowledge Quadrant, Maxine recognized that learning something new was always a stimulus for energy. She opted to take a course at the local community college. Maxine's burnout went away.

> **"When you learn to say yes to yourself,**
> **you will be able to say no to others,**
> **with love."** –ALAN COHEN

TAKING SPIRAL IMPACT TO THE MAT IN BUSINESS

APPLICATIONS FOR LEADERS AND TEAMS

Diversity of thought, talent, preferences, and experience is great for innovation; however, it can often create divisions for those not mastering conflict. How do we bring out the best in everyone to achieve the ultimate goals of innovation and highly engaged people? The following applications include training people in the Spiral Impact Method to create a base of understanding and common language.

In this section, you'll learn about:

- Giving Deliberate Feedback—Improving Performance
- Turning a Hot Mess into A Cool Breeze—Getting Clarity and Movement
- Aligning and Developing Teams—Cutting out the Honeysuckle

GIVING DELIBERATE FEEDBACK

When I teach *aikido*, and Spiral Impact, I want people to enjoy learning. People will disengage quickly if they feel beaten up by too much harsh feedback. Believe me I've had teachers that made me want to cry! On the other hand, if people get no feedback, they may not grow and improve.

Many leaders dread giving feedback. So they don't do it. Effective feedback that helps people improve their performance is priceless and, unfortunately, rare. So much feedback is given as a consequence of a negative event—getting fired or missing a promotion over something never communicated; on the *aikido* mat it could be a bruise! Let me share my take on feedback with the following story.

> *As I headed to a client meeting, I wove in and out through major road construction as if in a war zone. I thought to myself, "How ironic that construction is often is experienced as destruction!"*
>
> *As I began our coaching session my client said, "Giving constructive feedback is difficult for me."*

There was that word again: "Constructive." But my drive through the messiness of the road construction gave me a new context that helped me understand and acknowledge my client's difficulty:

Constructive feedback is often received as destructive.

I believe this is why most people feel uncomfortable giving feedback—it feels destructive. When caught in road construction, one way I cope is to imagine how nice this is going to be when it is finished. I focus on the improvement, the outcome. Or another way to say it on what is being constructed.

TIP: When you give feedback, shift your thinking from constructive to improving an outcome.

Feedback is constantly happening, whether you are aware of it or not. If you become deliberate in your feedback, you will never feel destructive again.

There are Three Forms of Feedback:

- Positive recognition
- Performance improvement
- Ending a relationship

If you are consistently deliberate with the first and second, the third either never happens—or at least it isn't a surprise when it does.

When giving deliberate feedback be consistent with Spiral Impact concepts, including asking questions, being centered, and focusing on desired outcomes or organizational impact.

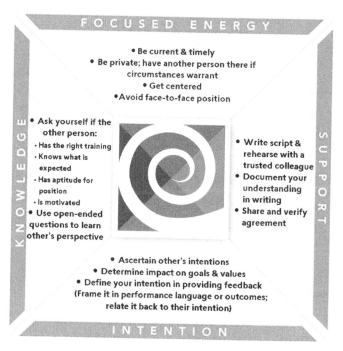

FIGURE 22: *Giving Deliberate Feedback Map*

When you give feedback in this way, you can help people reach their own conclusions and hold them accountable for agreed-upon behavior. Skip the destructive feelings and be comfortably deliberate with your feedback!

Begin with the Knowledge Quadrant and ask yourself the reflection questions. If the answer to any of these is no, address them before you provide feedback to someone.

Here is an example:
SITUATION: *Mark is a high technical performer; his people skills are terrible. He intimidates others and creates an awkward feeling in the department.*

REFLECTION:
- ☑ *Has the appropriate knowledge/training*
- ☐ *Knows what is expected*
- ☐ *Has the aptitude for the position*
- ☑ *Is motivated or invested in being there*

SUMMARY: *He is valued and very well trained technically, but not in soft skills. I've talked to him about being nicer, but he hasn't changed. I am not sure if he has the aptitude for working comfortably with other people.*

HOW DOES THIS IMPACT ORGANIZATIONAL GOALS? *People are scared to engage with him; innovation is stopped.*

HAVING THE CONVERSATION: *<First rehearse and get centered.>*

INTENTION: *"Mike, helping you succeed and accomplish your goals is important to me. And I'd like to talk with you about something in this regard. Is this okay?"*

KNOWLEDGE–DISCOVERY QUESTIONS:

- *"How do you best engage with your co-workers to solve problems?" <listen>*
- *"Does that work well?" <listen>*
- *"How do you encourage your co-workers to ask you questions and engage with you?" <listen>*
- *"Can you tell me more about that?" <listen>*

RESTATE INTENTION AS STATED ABOVE TO CREATE DESIRED OUTCOME:

- *"Your co-workers need to be comfortable approaching you with questions and requests for assistance."*
- *"Your role requires good communication skills. Are you open to improving in this area?" <listen>*

ACCOUNTABILITY:

- *"I've identified resources to assist you to make these changes. Are you open to and committed to improving in this area? <listen>*
- *I'd like to meet weekly to discuss progress."*

A handbook for providing deliberate feedback is available on:
www.karenvalencic.com/resources/.

TURNING A HOT MESS INTO A COOL BREEZE

When new people show up to the dojo to learn *aikido*, if they've practiced another martial art, they tend to move in ways that reflect how they've been trained. For example, *karate* tends to be much more linear and avoids falling down. It's different, and the body memory interferes with the speed of their progress as *aikido* artists.

The same is true in business organizations. Unless they're specially trained, people learn their communication strategies from what was modeled for and practiced by them before they were hired —often by their families and popular culture. For some people this is a good thing; for others, it's absolutely not.

In the popular culture—the news and entertainment cycles—dysfunctional conflict builds titillating drama that draws high ratings. In real life, this type of dysfunction is painful. In business, the drama has an enormous price tag in lost productivity, stunted innovation, and diminished health.

Organizations that see the value of investing in communication and team development before things go haywire are wise! Still, it is never too late. I frequently am asked to intervene when all else fails and people no longer want to talk with each other.

Einstein is attributed with saying, more than 75 years ago, "Problems cannot be solved by the level of thinking that created them." This still holds true, particularly in challenging communications.

Many people address conflict at the level it was created by rehashing and building more evidence for their "side" of an argument. Repeating a position tends to intensify the separation of people.

Let's get back to Einstein and how I see his quote in action.

There is a common belief that dealing with the "elephant" in the room solves a problem. In my experience dealing with the "elephant" is often a rehash of the initial thinking.

I frequently get calls from clients who try to deal with the elephant, by "getting everything on the table," only to find the problem is much bigger than the piece they're focused on. Let me give you an example:

Matt and Zack's working relationship had devolved into a toxic, unhealthy, hot mess. The spite they had for each other was contaminating everything within range. Their leaders had tried addressing the elephant with no success and just made it worse; so, they asked if I could help. These were two highly valued, intelligent employees. My usual response to these situations: "I can't guarantee kumbaya, but I can get clarity and movement."

Spiral Impact did, however, get to them to kumbaya; here is how.

First, I met with each of them, separately, confirming they each were "all in" to find a different way to relate. As I coached them in Spiral Impact skills, they began to see their contributions to the conflict. It's fun to experience the ah-ha as people suddenly realize what they're doing doesn't serve their intention or well-being. The practical nature of Spiral Impact quickly reveals sticking points.

Each of them began to trust me, individually. However, when it was time for the three of us to meet, they questioned my method. They thought the elephants in the room needed to be hashed out. The trouble was they'd already tried that. It didn't work.

To prepare for the meeting, I asked that they write out their intentions about their working relationship. Intention is what you want, not what you want someone else to do. There are three types of intentions explored in the Spiral Impact Model: big picture, immediate, and deeper personal. (Refer to Section 2, Intention Quadrant)

Matt and Zach began sharing their intentions. My ground rule was they listen and then, when addressing each other, they only ask questions. As they took turns sharing, I could feel the tension soften with the similarity of their intent. There was a palatable shift like a door opening to give way to a beautiful, reflective lake of calm and clarity. Time slowed down; emotions settled. Then, almost magically, they realized their spite toward each other had sprung out of a series of misunderstandings amplified over time by many, small projections of distrust.

Once the elephant was deflated enough, and the imagined issues were exposed, their ideas of how they productively wanted to work together were revealed and agreed upon.

BRINGING TEAMS INTO ALIGNMENT

Honeysuckle has a strong hold on my woods. As I continuously cut it back, I see such parallels to the work I do with teams and leadership development.

An unchecked invasive species like honeysuckle prevents native trees and wildflowers from growing into their strength and glory, resulting, over time, in a bramble of honeysuckle and dead trees.

Team culture is very much the same. Unless an organization's culture is clearly defined and held to account, the most dominant personality—good or bad—will rule. Negative culture can cause high performers to feel used, discourage new people from engaging at their best, and lower the performance of the whole team.

What do you do to create a magnificent team?

I find three things give the best results:

CHECK LEADERSHIP ALIGNMENT

A few years ago, I was asked to work with a leadership team whose director was upset because they were not nice to each other. I was taken aback when invited to an introductory meeting, and the director berated the team for not being nice to each other. I witnessed her modeling the behavior she didn't want from them! Needless to say, the director was part of the problem.

Leadership sets the lead. They will get what they model. As I begin an engagement, I make sure outcomes are defined, and ensuring the leadership is modeling the desired behavior is my first priority.

If there is split leadership, where two separate organizations lead, and they are not both aligned, engaged, and committed, the engagement likely will fail.

In the honeysuckle example, getting the leadership to align with one another and with the desired behaviors or outcomes is equivalent to committing to transforming the landscape. I often serve as the landscape architect.

TRAINING IN SPIRAL IMPACT TO MASTER THE ART OF CONFLICT

When individuals have the same understanding of conflict and language, team efforts leap forward. As the project continues and the team gets stuck, we point back to the keys of Spiral Impact, and they always work. In the honeysuckle example, here we are fertilizing the plants to be in their individual strength.

ENGAGE THE GROUP TO DEFINE THEIR CULTURE—CREATE A CREDO

At this point, the intention is set by leadership and tools for mastering conflict are in place. Now it's time to dialogue about how they'll engage with each other. This process is as important as the end product, which is a short list of "yes" or "no" questions—a credo they agree to. (Refer to Section 2, Intention, Four Questions.) I've worked with hundreds of teams, and each credo is unique to their culture and team dynamics.

To accomplish this, I've had great success using a modified Appreciative Inquiry process, which focuses on sharing what has worked in the past and a positive orientation to the future. Typically, I ask individuals to reflect on these three questions:

- Think about a time you were involved with a group of people and it was an enlivening experience. What was it? What made it such an expansive experience for you?
- What are your values? What are the organizational values?
- What three wishes do you have for this team? Make them about what you want, not what you don't want.

Then, we form smaller groups of five to seven people. Each group shares their answers to the questions, making notes on large flipchart paper. For the first question, I ask that they record common, relevant themes. After they are complete, we gather all the flipcharts to the front of the room and review them as a large group. I've done this with up to 150 people.

From this point, I ask the group to formulate closed ended questions. If they answer "yes" to any given question, they've addressed something important to the group. The goal is to have three to seven questions. Making them easy to remember is key. I suggest questions rather than statements because questions beg an answer. Value statements are static.

Often people will say the questions are common sense. Yes, they are. Often people don't communicate as they'd like others to—this is a commitment and guide to have everyone on the same page.

It is important to have everyone sign their name to commit to this credo as safeguard. This is a tool to always come back to when "honeysuckle" begins to grow.

Sometimes people decide to leave their jobs after we complete this process. As the conversation about culture ensues, people get clarity about whether the organization is the best place for them or not. It's good if they leave if they cannot agree with the group's credo. This is like cutting honeysuckle out by the roots!

Just like honeysuckle, if team culture isn't held in check to a certain standard, it runs wild. I've seen some of the toughest groups shift with these three simple strategies. I once worked with 12 teams who were in their company's lowest percentile of engagement and satisfaction, as measured by a third-party survey. When we defined their culture, 11 of the teams shifted to the highest percentile one year later. The one that continued to score low for engagement had split leadership who were not aligned.

SECTION 5

CLOSING THOUGHTS

CLOSING THOUGHTS ABOUT CIVILITY

Adding even a little heat to a tinderbox can ignite a raging fire. As of this writing, this metaphor bears consideration as our country and our world are filled with people who have polar-opposite viewpoints.

I've found myself wondering whether it is courageous or crazy to attempt a meaningful dialogue to bridge divides. As someone who desires to bring people together, I've had some success with this; I have also set some accidental fires.

Avoiding conversations about delicate matters can sometimes be a good idea. I think this is a given in work settings—just don't go there. Or, if you go in feeling like you need to set people straight or change their position—just don't go there. These actions simply deepen the divide.

If you desire to narrow the divide, I recommend a centered curiosity approach. Curiosity is naturally centered (the calm eye in the storm) because being curious isn't trying to force or change anything; it is just trying to learn. Curiosity is a very different mindset than out-rage, righteousness, or fear. So, for bridging divides to work, leave your fact-filled matches in their box because facts only add fuel to emotional communications. I know that is a hard statement to accept, but it is true.

Be curious when things don't jive with what you believe or expect. For example, when a statement of opinion is made "Those people have no right," be curious and ask, "Tell me more how you see that..." or "How do you experience that?" or "How do you see that looking ten years from now?" or "What is your understanding...?" By sincerely asking what the other person thinks you might learn new information.

At this point, you may be tempted to get your facts out. **DON'T DO IT!** Instead, ask another sincere question!

> *Just like buying a car...you want to explore all sides and the ins and outs! Nobody is forcing you to buy, and curiosity is not agreement.*

At some point, when you are satisfied that you genuinely understand, then introducing your ideas as questions may open the conversation. For example: "Have you considered <blank> as a possibility?" Or you might even agree to disagree: "I respect your views, although I see things differently."

In my experience, this is the best way to open a dialogue where you can invoke curiosity in the other person. Perhaps, they will be interested in your point of view! And, if it backfires, that's okay too.

Centered curiosity is courageous and promotes civility. Crazy throws more fuel on to the fire! Your choice.

(It's important to note that alcohol sabotages curiosity and is best kept at a distance from volatile situations.)

ANOTHER CLOSING THOUGHT

It took years to learn to do it well, but now I love doing it: falling.

Falling is a basic skill in *aikido*. Falling well is essential to protecting yourself. If done with a spiral movement, falling creates momentum that propels you back to your feet, ready for the next attack. Hesitate and you're likely to get hurt and stay on the ground longer.

We all take falls in life. That is a fact. Spiral Impact is a simple tool for when you feel stuck or in struggle. Use it and remember to "keep moving and bend those knees!"

> *Communication creates movement;*
> *Stillness fosters clarity.*
> *To be clear and moving,*
> *this is true power.*

I keep "moving and bend my knees," therefore I continually create new support materials. For the latest product and program information, I invite you to periodically visit my website, and better yet, sign up on the mailing list: WWW.SPIRALIMPACT.COM

ABOUT THE AUTHOR

Karen Valencic is passionate about revealing the keys to mastering conflict so leaders can fast-track innovation and smooth the turbulence of change—thereby increasing momentum!

If you've seen Karen present, you are likely to remember! Her sessions are uniquely grounded in martial arts and physics. Almost three decades of experience developing high-performing teams informs her content. Karen will soon be a 3rd-degree black belt in the martial art, *aikido*, and she is a degreed tenured mechanical engineer. She is the founder and president of Spiral Impact, a performance improvement company.

One of Karen's gifts is making complex concepts simple and entertaining. It deeply matters that her clients have immediately applicable, practical tools and have fun in the learning process.

Ready to master conflict and be on the path to freedom? Begin now!

 Go to: **https://karenvalencic.com/resources/**

ACKNOWLEDGMENTS

Support is priceless; so are the challenges, tough questions, and rejections. As I launch this Black Belt Edition and reflect how the content has evolved over the last 13 years, I have thousands of people to whom I say, "Thank you. Your questions and willingness to engage and challenge the content have made me and the process better."

My *aikido* training is at the core of my work and my life. A very special thank you goes to Joe Lavelle Sensei for his very direct feedback and support on the original book. Many thanks to: Thomas Crum for opening the *aikido* door and demonstrating how conflict is magical; George Bevins for giving me a strong base in the early years of my training; and Dave Johnson for his continued day-to-day teaching. I offer my gratitude, too, to the late Kevin Choate Sensei whose *aikido* teaching opened a much deeper practice for me in my 20th year: You are missed but live on in your students. Thank you, too, Hiroshi Ikeda Sensei and Mitsugi Saotome Sensei for generously sharing your *aikido* gifts; and, to all of my practice partners over the years. I'd also like to mention a newer influence, Lisa Tomoleoni Sensei: I've so enjoyed your teaching and look forward to much more.

Denise Dilworth has been a wonderful editor for this edition. I feel she gets 'It." Deb Hart May, my 1st Edition Editor, thank you for your gentle yet firm guidance and expertise. Wend Boomhower, my artist, thank you for your patience and creativity.

Also, special thanks to Jack, father of my daughters, for your impeccable support all of these years; and to my daughters, Kylie and Taylor, for sharing a wonderful, centered family base.

BRING A FRESH TWIST TO YOUR NEXT EVENT WITH SPIRAL IMPACT

Your attendees will be engaged throughout, as Karen Valencic blends concepts from martial arts, physics, and almost three decades of developing leaders and teams. Popular topics include:

In Power Together

Being in power together happens when people set aside force and bring forth the elements of True Power in their relationships.

Momentum at the Intersection of Change, Innovation, and Conflict

The world compels people to speed up, do more, create more. But going faster isn't the answer. Momentum is what builds power.

Mastering the Art of Conflict

Conflict is the spark that lights the fire of innovation. However, the flames of conflict can also destroy trust and vitality that are essential to bringing out the best in people to create high performing teams and successful relationships.

The Art of Influence or The Power to Get It Done with Grace

Why keep on pushing to make things happen? Instead, learn to harness the power of a spiral and practice the art of influence and grace.

Contact us.

We will evaluate and design the best experience for your needs!
Info@karenvalencic.com • www.spiralimpact.com

DiSCOVER THE POWER OF WE™

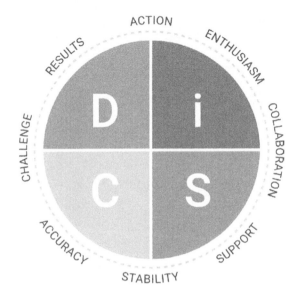

Unlock engagement, inspire collaboration, and ignite cultural transformation with Everything DiSC® and Spiral Impact® together. Everything DiSC® is an assessment-based learning experience that deepens self-awareness, inspires appreciation of others, and fosters effective collaboration in the workplace. Backed by over 40 years of research, you can expect customizable solutions that meet your organization's unique training needs. Start your organization on the path from personalized insight to cultural change today.

*Spiral Impact is in partnership with Everything DiSC®
because it is:*

- Built on a Foundation of Research and Rigor
- Simple but not Simplistic
- Customizable and Flexible

Contact us at: Info@karenvalencic.com

27230321R00115